ALL THE
DAYS OF
MY LIFE

(So Far)

ALISON SWEENEY

ALL THE DAYS OF MY LIFE

(So Far)

KENSINGTON BOOKS
www.kensingtonbooks.com

In this book, the author describes the weight loss and fitness program and the supplements that work best for her. She does not give professional advice or make any recommendations as to what regimen may be appropriate or advisable for others. Each individual should consult his/her own doctor prior to beginning any weight loss/exercise program and/or before taking any supplements.

KENSINGTON BOOKS are published by

Kensington Publishing Corp.
850 Third Avenue
New York, NY 10022

All Kensington titles, imprints, and distributed lines are available at special quantity discounts for bulk purchases for sales promotions, premiums, fundraising, educational, or institutional use.

Special book excerpts or customized printings can also be created to fit specific needs. For details, write or phone the office of the Kensington special sales manager: Kensington Publishing Corp., 850 Third Avenue, New York, NY 10022, attn: Special Sales Department; phone 1-800-221-2647.

Kensington and the K logo are Reg. U.S. Pat. & TM Off.

ISBN 0-7582-0609-7

First printing: June 2004

10 9 8 7 6 5 4 3 2 1

Printed in the United States of America

Designed by Leonard Telesca

To Mom and Papa, my intelligent and talented parents, who taught me to embrace life and always encouraged me to pursue my dreams.

Acknowledgments

In writing this book, I was reminded of those who have shaped my life and brought me personal happiness and professional success. Executive producer Ken Corday has always made *Days* more than just a workplace, but a family; I thank him and casting director Fran Bascom for making me part of such an amazing show. My *Days* family (cast and crew) has taught me so much, especially Deidre Hall, who from my first day on the set has been my mentor and my friend; and my favorite co-star Bryan Dattilo, who doesn't know how truly talented he is. With *Days* has come an incredible group of NBC executives whose support has led to more opportunities than I could have ever imagined.

Many people are fortunate to have even one strong support system; I've been blessed with several. A special thanks to my family—the Sweeneys, Gleasons, and Sanovs—especially Mom and Papa; my brothers, Ryan and Sten, who always encouraged me to soar but kept me grounded; my cousin Christy, the sister I never had; and Aunt Jane, whose wisdom, style, and friendship have always been invaluable to me.

Growing up, I aspired to have a circle of friends for life and I'm lucky to have found them: My best friend Carrie, with whom I share a brain, not to mention everything else in our lives; and Stephanie, Lauren, Shari and Ari are always with me, whether by phone or e-mail, in traffic or on a red carpet. *"I love us!"*

This book could not have been written without the advice, guidance, and support of my literary agent, Jane Dystel; my co-writer Richard Trubo, who transformed my stories into what I hope you'll find to be an interesting book; my publicist of eleven years, Charles Riley; and my editor (and *Days* fan), John Scognamiglio, who offered so many good suggestions to keep the book accurate and on target.

Saving the most important for last, my husband, Dave, has filled my life with love, laughter, understanding, and encouragement.

Like sands through the hourglass, I thank all of you for the days of my life . . . so far!

ALL THE
DAYS OF
MY LIFE

(So Far)

Chapter 1

"Like sands through the hourglass, so are the days of our lives . . ."

Sound familiar?

I've been serenaded by that opening mantra of *Days of Our Lives* for more than ten years now—and loving every minute of it. Since that January morning in 1993 when I walked onto the set of *Days* for the first time, I've taken a wonderful ride that is as exciting today as it was a decade ago.

For more than a third of my life, the Midwestern town of Salem has been home, and let me tell you, it's never been dull. Because you're reading this book, you're probably a *Days* fan, and perhaps even a fan of my amazing character, Sami Brady. I've been so lucky to play someone like her who millions of viewers love—or, to be more accurate, often love to hate.

Admit it—there are probably dozens of Sami moments that are indelibly imprinted in your own mind. She has survived a brutal rape, struggled with bulimia, given birth to a beautiful son, spent some terrifying moments on death row, kidnapped and tried to sell her own baby sister on the black market, was stranded at the altar (how many times now?), fought repeatedly and viciously with her mother (and just about everyone else in Salem!), lied about her son's paternity, and slept with her older sister's fiancé. All in a day's work! Yet through it all, Sami's still standing, still scheming, still devious and dangerous, and still winning the hearts, minds (and, let's face it) the animosity of the six million fans who watch the show each week and seem barely able to survive without their daily fix of *Days*. As the NBC Web site recently said, "Alison Sweeney has become pretty good at playing bad."[1]

I know what it's like to be a *Days of Our Lives* "addict." Before I joined the show, I was already happily hooked on *Days*. I had started watching the show during the summer vacation before the ninth grade, and once I returned to school in the fall, I set up the VCR each morning and taped every episode without fail. When I'd watch the show, it was the perfect way for me to "chill out" after school. The day-to-day turmoil in Salem provided the perfect escape from my own real-life dramas at school. *Days* was (and is) absolutely habit-forming.

So when I was chosen to play Sami in 1993, at the age of sixteen, I felt like the luckiest girl in the world. And in many ways, I still do. The writers of *Days* have created a character that you can't stop thinking about or trying to figure out. Even if some viewers don't want to admit it, many of them relate to her, even though she certainly isn't the most angelic character on daytime television.

1. You might be wondering why I refer to Sami in the third person throughout this book. Sami is a huge part of my life, and I love playing her. But Sami is her own person, and she and I are not one in the same. If you know her through the show, you'll understand why I keep her separate in my own mind.

(NBC)

While some *Days* watchers are absolutely baffled by Sami, others love her and are proud of being a "Sami-Fan." I am well known for surfing the Web and stopping by to visit and post at Sami-friendly sites. Still, hardly a week goes by when someone doesn't ask me skeptically, "Do you *really* like playing Sami?" In fact, I love Sami.

Okay, she does the kinds of unbelievably crazy things that are so outrageous. But admit it, she behaves the way that most of us have wanted to at one time or another, but never had the nerve.

Sami's saving grace is that her behavior—the good, the bad, and the ugly—comes from a genuine place. It's a product of her love for the people in her life, her own insecurities, and her unwavering determination to go after what she wants. You have to respect that about Sami. She's definitely someone who millions of people identify with and even secretly admire, even when her mean streak is creating havoc throughout Salem.

Okay, I admit it—there are moments now and then when Sami even makes my own skin crawl. At times, I even wonder what it would be like to play a heroine who warms people's hearts and souls. I may look like someone with "girl-next-door wholesomeness" (as *TV Guide* once described me), but I certainly don't play one on TV! So I get plenty of letters and e-mails from fans who need to get things about Sami off their chest. Almost to a person, there's very little holding back.

But that's what makes playing Sami so interesting. She's a character who everyone has an opinion about—and I think I've heard all of them from fans who stop me on the street or interrupt me between bites at restaurants. Some offer warm hugs, telling me how much they adore Sami. Occasionally, however, they'll give me a good tongue-lashing, or (in one unforgettable moment) swing a purse at me in disgust over Sami's eccentric behavior. Viewers have told me that they've actually thrown things at the TV screen when Sami becomes more than they can bear. The most common refrain: "Sami's a real bitch!"

Through it all, I still love portraying Sami. I think she's so much fun. At the same time, I adore every one of my fans, whether they love Sami or hate her. This book is for them and for you.

A Show Business Tale

In this book, you'll read my story. It is not only an account of my ten-plus years at the Burbank studio where *Days of Our Lives* is taped. It is also about my life offscreen—the good fortune that I've had and also how I've navigated over both the ordinary and extraordinary speed bumps that can derail you if you're not careful. Of course, from the outside looking in, it may seem as though I've had it all. Since my midteens, I've starred on one of TV's most popular daytime soaps, I'm living out my lifelong dream of being a successful actress, and both fans and critics have been generous with their compliments about my acting. *Time* magazine once called *Days of Our Lives* the "most daring drama" on daytime television, and Sami and I have been right in the middle of it for more than a decade. No complaints at all! In fact, sometimes I can't believe it! ☺

At the same time, as I've moved from my own adolescence into adulthood, my life and my problems have been no different than those of so many other girls and young women. Problems with friends. Concerns about weight. Balancing work and play. Being pulled in every possible direction, and not always the right ones. Discovering my inner self, exploring my beliefs, and shaping my values. Along the way, there has often been a disconnect between the storybook image of a TV actress and what the real world dishes out. Yes, I've been lucky to have a wonderful show business career and a so-called glamorous life. But guess what? Most of my life is just like the lives of millions of other girls and women—confronting insecurities, coping with shyness, dealing with everyday anxieties, at times preoccupied with the way I look, and (of course) obsessing about the number on the bathroom scale. For better or worse, I've done it all in the public eye, where the smallest piece of gossip can make its way into the tabloids and ruin your day.

As I write this book, I still feel young, and like I'm just starting out in some ways. At the same time, I know that I'm somewhat of a "veteran" on a network soap. I've done the math, and I've been on *Days* for more than a third of my life. And, if I'm still there at age thirty, it'll be exactly half of my life! But I still think of myself as a kid, and if you had seen my best friend and me at a recent Bon Jovi concert, you would have thought we were fourteen-year-old groupies. I can giggle and gossip with the best of 'em, and I never want to take myself too seriously or feel as though I can't do youthful things (like visiting Disneyland—the "happiest place on earth").

Of course, it has been interesting growing up in L.A., which may be a little crazier than finding your way into adulthood in many other parts of the country. But I think most of the societal pressures and standards aren't that different, no matter where you call home. How well I remember high school, where it always seemed that other girls had the perfect bodies and the perfect lives—perhaps because they were on the cheerleading squad or dated the cutest guys in the class. Sounds a little shallow and superficial, right? But those are the kinds of things that are important when you're a teenager. Years later as an adult, when you look back with a little perspective and maturity, you can see that no one's life is perfect. Everyone has challenges, and the issues that once seemed so important often become insignificant.

Hollywood's Weighting Game

In Hollywood, many of life's pressures become exaggerated, and they can become suffocating if you let them. Take weight, for example. That's right, that scary scale can affect your mood for the whole day or week or. . . . In a high-profile industry like show business, you can't escape the fact that most young actresses have waiflike bodies and wrist-sized waists, and have never met a diet they didn't like. I've met most of those same diets, too, and have been taken hostage by a few! But let me tell you, I've never felt much affection for any of them. Of course, America devours diets and the hottest new diet book on the block with infinite enthusiasm (do the names Atkins, Sears, and Ornish ring a bell?), and for as long as I can remember, I was often consumed with my weight, even though I was never terribly heavy. In high school, during those times when I tipped the scales at a little more than I'd like, I might find myself overcome with doubts that I just wasn't pretty enough or that I wasn't going to be attractive to boys (welcome to adolescent anxiety!).

On my home turf—Hollywood—dieting has been taken to another level. For many actresses, it has become an obsession that borders on the maniacal. I won't say that I've never bought into this "Honey, I Shrunk the Actress" mindset. In fact, for many years, even though I was never obese, I tried fitting into a culture that reveres lean, angular bodies in women, and for a long time I really became fixated on my weight. In this book, I'll tell you about my struggles—how I became one of the sweating masses crowding into trendy health clubs in L.A. . . . how I went on a dozen or more absolutely crazy diets . . . how I ate only fruit . . . tried not eating after 5 P.M. . . . ordered meals that were prepared by nutritionists and delivered to my door. But nothing worked very long. Absolutely nothing.

Sounds insane, doesn't it? It really was a sad and pathetic way to live, diet after diet, year after year. Frankly, I get exhausted just thinking about it. Yet more than once, casting directors told me that I didn't get a particular role— perhaps for a "Movie of the Week"—because "you're just too fat for the part." Ouch! Yep, they really can be that brutally honest!

But here's the real tragedy: After a while, I began believing them. I absolutely hated myself when I glared at the scale and it glared back at me with unwelcome news. There were even a few times when I felt such despair that I wanted to throw up my hands and say, "Forget Hollywood! Maybe I'll do something else with my life. I don't need this agony." There were desperate moments when I just wanted to stop at Krispy Kream on the way home from the studio and curl up in bed with a dozen doughnuts instead of the next day's script. But as you'll read, "giving up" on my weight or anything else just isn't who I am.

Turning Points

Before we go on, let me make this clear: This certainly isn't a diet book. As I tell my own story, I'm *not* going to advise you on what to eat and when to eat it. Far from it. A nutritionist or dietician can handle that much better than I can. But I hope you'll find some inspiration when you read about my own turning points, finally overcoming the struggles with an issue that got too much of my attention for much too long. Whether you live in California or Canada, New York or New Mexico, we all watch the same television shows and read the same fashion magazines, which leave most women thinking that we shouldn't have eaten that yummy slice of cheesecake the night before or allowed our jogging shoes to collect dust in the closet. *US Weekly*, *Women's World*, VH1, *Entertainment Tonight* and *E! Entertainment* have documented my own dieting efforts. Even so, diets no longer dominate my life 24/7. And with a more relaxed attitude, my excess weight really has disappeared and certainly isn't the issue it once was.

But still, let's be honest: Wherever I go, people are *always* talking about losing weight. It's been over five years since I went through my own significant weight loss, but still I can hear their words echoing through my mind—"How many calories is that?" . . . "No, thanks, that food isn't on my diet." . . . "Does this outfit make me look fat?" . . . Then there's my favorite, sometimes said with tongue in cheek: "Don't you absolutely *hate* her—she can eat anything she wants."

It's an insane way to live!

Fortunately, as I'll describe in these pages, a lot of my actress-friends and I have developed a much healthier outlook, recognizing just how ridiculous the weight game can be. We're very clear that the attention on our waistlines and the bathroom scale can be curses for Hollywood actresses and women everywhere. But I'm also clear about another thing: Since I had my first Kodak moment on a TV commercial when I was just five years old, acting has been my dream. I'm good at it. I'm certainly passionate about it. It's what I know and what I love. So I've made a conscious decision to remain strong, fight back, and try to stay above the fray and the need to fit the stereotypical mold of the perfect actress with the perfect figure.

Yes, I've waged a lot of internal psychological warfare over the years, and I've tried shifting the focus away from the scale and more toward leading a happy, healthy, fulfilling life. Of course, I still watch what I eat, and I'm always weighing my options when I'm reading a menu or shopping in the supermarket. But as you'll read in this book, I'm not the fanatic I used to be. I know that my body type will never allow me to look like the next Kate Moss or any other supermodel, for that matter.

But here's the amazing part of this story: The producers of *Days of Our Lives* have never made an issue of my weight. I'm so lucky to work for people who are so supportive. Whether I've been a little overweight or just right, they have only been interested in creating a great character who fans love—or hate! It really hasn't mattered what I weigh.

Sami's Longevity

Years ago, when I joined the cast of *Days of Our Lives*, I never could have imagined that I'd be sitting here, over a decade later, having gone through adolescence and young adulthood in the public eye and still having the privilege of playing Sami. So many soap characters come and go quicker than you can strike the delete button on a scriptwriter's computer. Characters are done in by diseases, laid to rest by jealous lovers—or they sometimes just "go upstairs" and are never heard from again. But somehow Sami has survived every transgression and every misstep—and she's had plenty of them. When I won a fan-voted Emmy award in 2002, do you remember the category? It was "America's Favorite Villain," of course. The award was custom-made for Sami!

Sure, Sami may never be the girl who guys dream of bringing home to mom. But many fans have looked beyond her character flaws—and beyond Sami herself—and have turned me into their sounding board and perhaps even role model. Every week, I receive hundreds of letters and e-mails, some from fans who just want to give Sami or me a piece of their mind. But others ask for my advice on "girl concerns" that are important in their lives. Why me? Here's what I think: Every afternoon on *Days*, I come into their living rooms, and many of them feel that I'm part of their family (no kidding!). They confide in me. They describe their own relationships with parents and friends, husbands and boyfriends. They recount their personal stories of dating, marriage, and sex . . . and of weight gain and weight loss. They even sometimes say, "Ali, I don't

know why I'm writing to you—I really don't know you—
but I feel like I can talk to you more honestly than to most
other people in my life."

Later in this book, I'll include some of the letters and
e-mails I've received from fans. Many of them are quite remarkable and very touching. When fans have written to
me about confronting their insecurities, seeing themselves
in a new way, and building their own self-confidence—and
they give some of the credit to me because of inspirational
things I've said in the media—they've motivated me to
write this book, to tell my story, to share my experiences
on *Days*, and I hope, to infuse them (and you) with some
additional encouragement to be courageous, to be bold,
and to follow your dreams.

When I respond to fan mail, I often tell viewers that
while my life may seem glamorous, I'm really just like them.
I haven't escaped any of the pressures and anxieties experienced by virtually every girl or woman. No matter where
you live or what your life circumstances are, I'm convinced
that all of us should strive for happiness by enjoying old
friendships and creating new ones, embracing our families,
and nurturing the love in our lives. I hope you'll search for
who you really are, and accept yourself with all of your
good qualities as well as your shortcomings. Set meaningful goals and work hard to reach them.

Of course, in this book you won't catch me claiming
that I have all the answers. But like Sami, I've learned a lot
and I go after what I want. Whether it's setting my sights
on an acting role or learning to play racquetball with my
husband, Dave, my expectations have always been high. I
enjoy challenges and doing some out-of-the-box thinking

about goals and how to reach them. That's where the fun of living can be.

Like so many actors, I'm following my dreams and my heart. I've never been the kind of person to sit at home, waiting for the phone to ring or for the world to come to me. I go after what I want—and I hope I'll inspire you to do the same! I keep my eyes open to everything the world has to offer, and I try to make things happen, developing my talents and working to excel at every opportunity.

At the same time, I've also become better at finding balance in my life. As Dave and my girlfriends will tell you, I take time just to hang out "away from the office." I try not to spread myself too thin. A life without balance isn't genuine, and I'm enjoying life more as I become older.

Navigating Through the Book

So turn the page and let's get started. I hope you'll enjoy reading about my experiences—all the rewards, all the challenges—as well as life on the set of *Days of Our Lives*. I'll tell you about the other actors on the show . . . recollections of my most memorable scenes . . . and everything you always wanted to know about Sami. At the same time, even though my own profession may be different than yours, I think you'll find a lot in these pages that will remind you of times in your own life. Growing up, I've yearned for friends, ached to have love in my life, felt overwhelmed at times by the pressures and stresses, and struggled with the scale. Welcome to Life 101!

After reading my story, you might be inspired by the

journey that I've taken. I may light a fire that encourages you to follow your own dreams. More than anything, I want you to enjoy this book, and through my story, find yourself motivated to live in rhythm with the person you are and want to become.

Chapter

2

(Author's personal collection)

Salem's Future Hellraiser!

In some ways, playing Samantha Jean Brady is like wearing an old comfy pair of jeans that I can put on anytime, anywhere, knowing that they'll fit perfectly. After more than a decade, I know Sami so well that sometimes I think I know what she's going to do and say, even without looking at the script.

When the producers of *Days of Our Lives* hired me in 1992, they told me that I was the perfect fit to play Sami. There had been previous incarnations of the character,

(Jon McKee)

played by five different child actors (from Ronit Aronoff to Christina Wagoner), dating back to 1984. But now the producers and writers had decided to bring Sami back as a teenager. What a wonderful opportunity for the actress who would get the part!

When my agent told me about the auditions, I was skeptical about my chances. After all, I know what the odds are in this industry. You may know that dozens and sometimes even hundreds of actors often try out for a single part. You've probably heard about the "cattle calls." The stories are true. So it's smart not to get your hopes up too high.

At the time, I certainly didn't fit the stereotype of the typical underweight, undersized, undernourished actress. See, I was a little overweight (especially by Hollywood standards)—maybe by about ten to fifteen pounds at the most. It was nothing to be particularly concerned about—unless you're an actress. If you think America is obsessed with its waistlines, just try show business on for size. This is a community and a profession where the anthem seems to be that you can never be too slender.

Fortunately, however, the producers of *Days* had something else in mind when casting Sami. Of course, Sami is Marlena Evans' (Deidre Hall's) daughter and Carrie's (Christie Clark's) younger sister, and the soap's writers already had a story line in the works for their new addition to the cast. They were considering a story line where Sami would battle bulimia, the binging-purging eating disorder that affects millions of Americans, mostly adolescent girls and young women. As a result, the producers were thinking outside the box when searching for the next Sami. They weren't necessarily seeking a razor-thin actress who looked like she had never craved a Godiva chocolate or never had a weakness for French pastry. (As one magazine noted when describing the search for an actress to play Sami, "Most soaps would have cast a glammy, reed-thin sexpot in such a conspicuous role.") Later, I found out that their "job description" for Sami was simple yet demanding—a young actress who could carry her own weight (so to speak) with the rest of the cast. Everything else was secondary.

Yet when I first heard that *Days* was casting Sami, I was baffled. After all, I was already a big fan of the show, and at the time, Marlena didn't have a sixteen-year-old daughter on the show, or at least I had never seen her. So what the heck was this audition all about?

Well, when I got the script for the tryout, the mystery

was solved. Here's what I learned: The very young Sami was being aged, and she was about to reemerge as a key character on the show. What a cool idea! I couldn't have been more excited. I *really* wanted this part.

The Tryout

I was a bundle of nervous energy leading up to the audition. When the day finally arrived—a Monday afternoon after school—I drove to the interview, which was with Fran Bascom, *Days'* casting director. Fran, who is still in charge of casting for *Days*, is a great lady, and I was really anxious about meeting her. But she was so nice that, almost right away, I felt much more comfortable. As for the reading itself, I certainly did my best but wasn't really sure how well (or how poorly) I had done.

As I was walking out the door, Fran stopped me in my tracks and pulled me aside. "Ali," she said, "you did a great job."

A great job?! Wow! Believe me, you don't usually hear that kind of positive feedback at an audition. It just doesn't happen. Usually, it's just an emotionless "thank you" or something equally vague so that you leave having no idea whether they hated you or loved you. Normally, you have to wait a few days, and you don't hear back directly, but rather through your agent or manager.

"Look," Fran continued, "we're holding the screen test on Wednesday. Ali, I want you to come back on Wednesday. Can you make it?"

Was she kidding or what?! I couldn't believe Fran was telling me this right then and there. She seemed to have instantly made a decision that I might be right for the part. I was so excited—and absolutely stunned.

"Definitely," I told her, desperately clinging to my composure. "I'll be there."

On the way home, I was so ecstatic—but so nervous—that I could barely think. Homework would have to wait. So would everything else except learning my lines for Wednesday's screen test.

I couldn't believe this was really happening.

I called my friend Mary that night. She was also a fan of *Days*, and I told her what had happened. We were both screaming and freaking out over the phone (I'm sure our parents—not to mention the neighbors—thought we had completely flipped out!). For the moment at least, I was on cloud nine!

The Screen Test

Then I had to think about the screen test.

I went to school on Tuesday and Wednesday, but I can't tell you much of anything that happened there. I spent every free moment reading and re-reading the script that would be used in the screen test. For forty-eight hours, butterflies fluttered in my stomach. I can assure you that I didn't sleep much on Monday and Tuesday nights. How could I, with my mind running wild with images of everything that might happen during the screen test—and what it would be like if I actually got the part?!

One really important way for me to prepare for the screen test was to schedule an appointment with my acting coach. I am a firm believer in coaches, and I still take acting classes today (I'll write more about this later). Having another eye to read the material and scrutinize my performance helped me lock down the character and also gave me the confidence to do my best in front of the cameras.

I carried the "sides"—which is what they call the audition scene—around with me everywhere. I'd sneak it out during chemistry (I was terrible at chemistry anyway) and review the notes I'd made during my coaching session. I swear, those were the longest two days of my life, waiting for that screen test!

At 3:30 on Wednesday afternoon, I arrived at the NBC studios in Burbank. I was so nervous. And so excited. I knew my lines but didn't know how much my nerves might affect my performance. I also knew that I had plenty of competition: At the studio, four other actresses were there, all of us being screen-tested for the part of Sami.

After I had my makeup applied, a stage manager told me to wait in an empty dressing room until my name was called. So I sat and waited. And waited. 4 o'clock. 4:30. 5:00. 5:30. More nervous. More excited. More waiting.

Finally, at 6 P.M., the stage manager called me and the other actresses to the set we'd be using, right next to the one for *Days*. The soap had just finished taping for the day, and the director was finally ready for our screen test. After talking to us for a few moments, he walked all of us through the scene, telling us where we'd be standing and how we'd be moving when we spoke our lines.[2]

Then Patrick Muldoon (ex-Austin) and Christie Clark (ex-Carrie) walked in. Just seeing them almost took my

---

2. This process is known as dry-blocking. "Blocking" is the technical term for the physical moves the director gives you during a scene, and "dry" because it's just the actors and the directors—no cameras.

breath away, and ratcheted up my nervousness a notch or two. What a thrill to meet them, not to mention to do a scene with each of them! I was so embarrassed to meet Patrick in particular—I had such a crush on him from watching the show. I blushed to the tips of my ears, and even the thick makeup couldn't hide it. In fact, Joe, one of our stage managers, still teases me about it today!

The other girls and I had the amazing experience of rehearsing our scenes with Patrick and Christie, and I somehow got through it. Then Joe told us to go back to the dressing rooms for some more waiting until it was finally our time before the cameras. All the actresses auditioning for the role were given separate "call times" and different rooms, so I never got a chance to talk to any of them. It was such an awkward situation, to know they were competing against me, but still needing someone to share the experience with. All the waiting was killing me (of course since then, I've grown very accustomed to waiting—it's practically in the job description).

I wouldn't have guessed I could become so tense and so starstruck at the same time, but I managed it when I spotted Lisa Rinna and a few other actors on the show. I was too embarrassed to introduce myself or say anything to them, but I do remember thinking how incredible it would be to work on the same show with them. For some reason, I still didn't expect to get the part, but it was so exciting for me just to be there, to spend time on the set, and to see some of *Days'* cast members. I had to pinch myself and wonder, "Could this really be happening to me?"

So, you're asking, how did the screen test go? Funny, but I really thought I might have blown it. Big time. The cameras were almost ready to start rolling for my scene with Patrick. That's when the stage manager said to me, "Don't forget to close the door behind you after you enter the scene."

Close the door? That wasn't in the script!

I suddenly started to become unglued. What if I forgot to close the door? Or what if I didn't close it just right? What if the door slammed? Could it cost me the job? Don't mess this up, Ali.

Patrick sensed that I was starting to melt down.

"Don't worry about the door," he told me gently. "It's not a big deal."

I managed a smile. Patrick's words were very comforting. He was so reassuring and the pressure lifted a little. I felt back in control. And, guess what? I *did* close the door. It *didn't* slam. And, of course, I got the part!

Waiting for the News

After Wednesday's screen test, I returned to school for the rest of the week, sitting on pins and needles waiting for word from the studio. They seemed like the longest days of my life.

On Friday, my agent finally got a call from the producers saying that I'd been hired. My agent contacted my mom, who immediately called my high school. Minutes later, when my classmates and I were filing out of my geometry class, one of the office assistants met me at the classroom door and handed me a note.

"From your mom," it read. "You got it!!"

Yes, there were two exclamation points at the end of the note. I felt like adding a thousand more.

My reaction? I was almost delirious. I screamed. I literally jumped for joy. I almost couldn't control myself. (Hey, I was 16 years old!)

So just how good was I on that screen test? Obviously, good enough to get the part. But let me put it in perspective: A few years ago some of the *Days* cast got together in my dressing room and we watched the videotapes of all of our screen tests, which Austin Peck (who played Austin Reed after Patrick Muldoon) had tracked down in the *Days* video library. Oh, my goodness! We were so bad!! Every one of us! We roared with laughter watching those tapes. Bryan Dattilo (Lucas) got some ribbing over the short gym shorts he wore on his videotape. I laughed so hard over how my bouncy walk had my "Jan Brady" hair swinging all over the place. We teased Austin about how different his voice sounded . . . well, the list goes on and on. Julianne Morris (ex-Greta), Arianne Zuker (Nicole) and I couldn't get over the now-out-of-fashion clothes that we wore with pride in the early '90s. It's not one of those videos that you want to share with the world.

But here's the good news: We were able to laugh at ourselves because we had grown so much as actors since we had auditioned for *Days*. That's one of the blessings of working on a soap. You're acting all the time, one day after another, with new opportunities to refine your acting abilities and develop your talent. Here's the way I think about it: As a soap actor, you know that even if you're unhappy with your performance in today's episode, you always have tomorrow to make things better (even though today's episode might continue to bug you for a while!). Because you're acting so much and so often, you're always growing and always learning something new about yourself and the craft of acting. When you look around you and recognize how talented the cast and crew are, you realize everyone there is at the top of his or her profession, and they all have something to teach you if you're willing to learn. Not only that, but your character is developing and changing as well, which continuously presents you with new acting challenges and demands. And the twists and turns in Sami's life have never allowed me to become blasé about playing her.

Into the Fire

On January 6th, 1993, I began my new life as a cast member of *Days of Our Lives*. What a day!

If you thought I was nervous for the screen test, you should have seen me on that first day of playing Sami. I was absolutely petrified. Shortly after I arrived at NBC, I got a tour of the set, and was introduced to the cast. Everyone—and I do mean everyone—was so friendly and supportive, to my great relief. I don't know why I was anticipating anything else, but being the new kid on the block, I just wasn't sure if I'd fit in and how I'd be accepted.

Well, those fears were certainly unfounded. The cast embraced me, and everyone behind the scenes—from the makeup people to the stage crew—couldn't have been any nicer. In no time at all, I felt like part of the family. But still, do you know what worried me the most? In the first few days, I was scared stiff that I'd accidentally call the actors by their characters' names. (Can you imagine me introducing myself to Matt Ashford, and calling him "Jack"?) Those are the kind of embarrassing scenarios that created some sleepless nights.

During that first week, I got my feet wet in a few scenes, but without a lot of dialogue. In fact, Sami was introduced slowly to the TV audience, and (as you might expect of Sami) in a most peculiar way. In fact, in the viewers' first glimpse of her, she was lurking around Salem, shrouded in a dark hat and coat. She made a phone call . . . but did not utter a word. I didn't even have to put on makeup for those scenes, since there was only a shot of my arm, or a camera angle from behind my shoulder, keeping me concealed in shadows. From the start, Sami was a mysterious character. Millions of *Days'* fans must have been asking themselves, "Who is this person and what is she doing in Salem?"

On the third day, Sami turned up at her parents' home. She peered under the doormat, but didn't find a house key there. So she removed her hat, pulled a bobby pin from her long, blonde hair, and used the bobby pin to break into her parents' house. Sami's father, Roman (played by Wayne Northrop at the time), heard the commotion that Sami was creating, and grabbed his gun. He snuck around the side of his house, confronted Sami in the shadows, pointed his gun at her and shouted, "Don't move."

Sami froze. After a few tense moments, I spoke my first words on *Days:*

"Daddy, don't shoot me!"

Fortunately, Roman didn't fire the gun. If he had, my career on *Days* may have ended right then and there.

A Little Help from My Friends

Ironically, in my first few months of playing Sami, she gave no hint of becoming the sassy (and, let's face it, sometimes obnoxious) character that she turned out to be. In fact, in those early days, Sami was a sweet, "good girl," and Marlena (played by Deidre Hall) and Sami had a close, loving relationship. But I've had to remind die-hard fans about Sami's innocent beginning many times—*how could they forget?* I ask myself! ☺ As it turns out, the writers of *Days* had originally created Sami as an innocent, naïve girl who may have felt a little inferior to her peers. Before long, however, she began to create chaos throughout Salem, one show after another, one year after the next. Early on, one of the prop guys and I would sometimes joke that there were two kinds of people in Salem—those who were given the key to the city, and the others who were given a bobby

(Lesley Bohm)

pin to pick any lock that got in their way; as Sami proved in that first week, she was definitely gifted with bobby pins!

From the beginning, I was lucky to be surrounded by actors on the set of *Days* who were not only talented, but were always generous with their advice and guidance. I learned so much just by watching the seasoned cast working around me. What a wonderful experience to be in scenes with actresses like Deidre (Marlena), who is not only brilliant at what she does, but has always been willing to offer suggestions and words of wisdom. It's amazing how quickly you can learn in that kind of environment. From the start, working with Deidre has given me an incredible opportunity to grow as an actress.

Looking back, I was actually a little hesitant at first to ask questions of someone of the stature of Deidre, who created the role of Marlena in 1976 (she once described her role on *Days* as "my longest-lived relationship"). But then I figured, "Which would be more embarrassing—to ask Deidre a foolish question, or to make a foolish mistake with the cameras rolling?" The answer to that one was obvious, so I asked again and again—and she couldn't have been nicer (and always has been!). I think Deidre could see that I was interested and eager to learn. So she was always receptive, always helpful, and definitely someone I knew I could turn to. She'd offer advice ("Why not try saying it this way?"), or give me an open-ended invitation to grill her with any question I had ("If you feel you don't get anything, just ask").

It may seem silly, but when you're a teenager and new to the show, you're afraid of what you don't know. On *Days*, however, there were always people to turn to for advice. And as far as Deidre goes, I've always loved acting in scenes with her, even when our characters were fighting. She has always made it easy.

A Juggling Act

When I joined the cast of *Days*, I found myself with more challenges than just adapting to the demands of playing Sami Brady. Along with this wonderful opportunity to chase my dream of an acting career, at age 16 I still needed to make school my first priority. Both goals were worth pursuing. My challenge was to create room for both school and acting in my life.

At the beginning, I figured that I'd work one day a week on *Days*, maybe less. My contract stipulated a commitment of at least half a day a week on the show, and I didn't expect to be doing much more. After all, I had been a fan of *Days*, and I had noticed that the child actors weren't on it very often, particularly during the school year. But the producers caught me by surprise. In no time, I learned that the scriptwriters had big plans for Sami. Almost from the start, she was a key player in the story lines of *Days*, requiring me to adapt to a three-day-a-week schedule. Fortunately, my schoolwork wasn't a casualty of the increased demands on my time—and I loved the challenge of juggling the two.

I was so fortunate that my own high school—a private school in the L.A. area—couldn't have been more accommodating. My teachers were thoroughly understanding and supportive of my career, and they made every effort to make sure I didn't fall behind. If I needed help after school, the teachers were always there. If I had questions, they patiently answered every one of them.

On the set of *Days*, the producers were just as supportive of my academics. They provided me with a teacher (by law, they have to do so, allowing minors to spend at least three hours a day on schoolwork while on the set). They even hired a special tutor to help me with my chemistry homework because (yes, let's face it) chemistry was not my strong suit.

At the time, the *Days'* daily schedule was very demanding for both the actors and the crew. Although our timetable has changed since then, the entire cast arrived at the studio sometime between 6 and 8 A.M. (ugh!) to prepare for what's called a "dry block" through the script, which I explained a little at the bottom of page 20. ("Blocking" is the physical movement in a scene—and when Sami decides to turn away from Lucas and move over to the table in the corner, that's called a "cross"; so in "dry blocking," the director will tell me that on a specific line, I am supposed to "cross" stage left. Is this making sense?)

At 8 A.M., we'd "camera block" the entire show, which means that the actors act out the scenes one by one so the cameramen and the rest of the crew know exactly where we'd be positioned during taping later in the day. The cameramen have to know where we're standing, and on which spoken lines we'll move, and the audio department needs to know where we'll be standing when we speak, so they can be sure to hear us! This rehearsal or "run through" of the day's entire show lasted until lunchtime.

After a meal break (which was also time to apply our makeup, touch up our hair, and change into our wardrobe), we'd move into a dress rehearsal of the show, and then wait for notes from the producers, which might include suggestions for script changes for the final taping. By 3 o'clock, the taping would begin, which might take three or more hours from beginning to end. It was a very long, very full day—but it was not over yet. I'd head home for an evening of homework—and learning my lines for the next show.

This schedule was so rigorous that it could wear you out if you didn't pace yourself. Imagine being on the set from early morning 'til night, squeezing in at least three hours of academic work somewhere during the day, and then catching up on any remaining schoolwork at home. I don't know how it all worked out, but it did. The studio teacher was always nearby, ready to work with me in-between rehearsals and during any other free moments during the day.

But as exhausting as my life may have seemed, I really think school itself had prepared me for it. Think back to your own middle school and high school years, when you'd attend classes for a full day and then spend hours doing homework at night. That kind of schedule can run you ragged, too, even without trying to squeeze in a day of acting. So it never really felt like an impossible transition from full-time student to full-time student/actor—except, that is, for one added source of anxiety that often disrupted my nighttime sleep. I began having nightmares—the kind of nightmares where you awaken startled and a bit panicky. The dream was always the same: I'd sleep through my alarm, wake up late, and rush to the studio, disheveled and scared to death that I had kept everyone else waiting. It was a terrifying dream, and ever since, I've always been petrified of being late to the set. The morning "calls" or reporting times were so early that oversleeping seemed like a real possibility (or in my case, perhaps a likelihood!). Even today, if I "sleep in" until 8 A.M. on a day off, I still wake up a bit stunned and disoriented, convinced that I'm late for work until I can figure out where I am and what day it is.

Except for minor inconveniences like that, my career on *Days of Our Lives* has been a wonderful part of my life, and the cast and crew have become very important to me. Even so, I knew that acting was "in my blood" for years before Sami Brady entered my life. In the next chapter, I'll take you back to my earliest moments in front of the cameras.

Chapter 3

How long have I known that I wanted to be an actress? Just about forever.

I think I might have been born with a passion for performing. I'm a native of Los Angeles, and I grew up in a musical household (my mom is a concert and studio musician who filled our home with classical music every day). I took the obligatory violin lessons and studied the violin seriously for eight years before I realized that my real love was acting—and I guess my mom realized it, too.

With my mother's support, I auditioned for and landed roles in many TV commercials. The first one was for Kodak film when I was just four years old. But if you're thinking that my talent was immediately recognizable to the world in that first acting experience—well, not exactly. I didn't have any lines to memorize, and frankly, the weather didn't exactly make it a magical experience. Although the ad depicted a winter scene, it was shot under a scorching 103-degree sun in L.A. But not to let sizzling

(Author's personal collection)

Daddy's
Little Girl

(Author's personal collection)

Virtuoso in
training!

weather interfere with the winter fun, the undaunted ad agency shipped in a truckload of snow to create a Hollywood version of a snow bank. Bundled up in a little red snowsuit, I climbed aboard a sled with my on-screen dad, and on the director's command of "Action," we rode down the slope while photos were being snapped of us (Kodak photos, I'm sure!). It was an all-day shoot, and as one take followed the next, the temperature became ever more blistering. But the show must go on, right? The prop guys worked overtime, frantically hauling in fresh snow to reinforce the man-made "mountain" that was melting under us. It was *very* hot, and the snowsuit sure didn't help! In fact, I almost passed out from heat exhaustion!

Despite the boiling sun, despite the snowsuit, and despite what others might call a nightmare day, I do remember this: I *really* had fun. I absolutely loved making that commercial. I somehow knew even then that acting would be something I'd do for the rest of my life. There wasn't a doubt. Some people are just lucky to be born knowing what they want and having the drive to pursue it. I guess I'm one of them.

A Word from Our Sponsor . . .

In the next few years, I took some commercial acting classes and went on a lot of auditions. By the time I was ten years old, I had appeared in about sixty TV ads. Some were as challenging as the hours on the snow slopes under a red-hot California sun; others were a breeze. Let me tell you about a few of my more interesting experiences.

When I was about six years old, I appeared in a McDon-

(Author's personal collection)

Wasn't I cute?!

ald's commercial. In it, four other girls and I were sitting in a McDonald's restaurant, eating French fries and giggling. Not too demanding, right? Well, at least not until the director ordered one take after another after another—requiring us to eat one handful of French fries after the next. You can imagine what happened. I was almost sick to my stomach by the end of the shoot. Now believe me, I think McDonald's has the best fries around. But I ate so many of them that I was feeling pretty ill that night at home. I don't think I had another French fry for about a year after that! Can you blame me?

Then there was a memorable commercial for Chewy Chips Ahoy. I was eight years old, and it was a two-day shoot, filmed by a lake more than two hours out of L.A. My "call time" was something crazy like 5 A.M., and I remember my mom having to wake me up at 2 in the morning to make sure we got there on time. I had only one line in the commercial, but there were a lot of different scenes—one of me eating cookies at a picnic, another of me eating cookies with my on-camera mom somewhere else in the park, and so on. You get the picture. Plenty of scenes. Plenty of cookies. If I had a cookie craving at the beginning of the day, it was *gone* by early afternoon.

When I was asked to appear in a second Chewy Chips Ahoy commercial, I guess I had forgotten just how demanding it can be to devour cookies virtually nonstop for a day or two. We did fifty takes of that second commercial—yes, fifty—each one requiring that I take a few bites of a Chewy Chips Ahoy cookie. This time, however, the director must have had visions of stomachaches sabotaging his commercial. So, he insisted, "Instead of swallowing the cookies, as soon as I yell 'cut' spit them into a bucket."

You've got to be kidding! At first, I resisted. But the prop guy kept warning me, "You'll wish you had." It didn't take me long to realize that he was right. I probably ate only five cookies that day—and spit out 45 more! Fortunately, the bucket never appeared in the commercial itself. It was pretty disgusting.

Nabisco promotes their cookies with the phrase "Ooey gooey warm 'n chewy." At the time, I'm not sure if I would have described it quite that way. They are delicious cookies—however, after hours of eating (and spitting out) cookies, I must have worked myself into a sugar frenzy that took a week or two to wear off!

The message, my friends, is that even a dream job like

eating cookies may require biting off more than you can chew. The same goes with feasting on ice-cream cones all day long. In one commercial, three little girls and I were supposed to walk through the park, licking ice cream cones. Sounds great so far. But it also happened to be a very hot day, and the director knew the ice cream wouldn't survive a single take, much less a day's worth of shooting. So he ordered the ice cream back into the freezer, and replaced it with "mashed potato cones," with the mashed potatoes dyed green! Sounds delicious, doesn't it? It wasn't exactly a child's *crème de la crème* dessert. But I made the best of it. As it turned out, we taped about forty takes, licking green mashed potatoes and pretending to enjoy every morsel. Now that's acting!

Child Acting 101

I'm so lucky to have always had an amazing and supportive family. From the earliest days, they encouraged my interest in acting without pushing me in one direction or another. My mom was always there to drive me to auditions, but she certainly didn't fit the stereotype of the pushy stage mom. She let me take the lead, and she always said that if I didn't want to go on auditions anymore, all I had to do was say so. With all that driving my mom had to do, going to and from auditions across town every other day, she would have been happy for me to call it quits at any time. She certainly never let the acting get in the way of my schoolwork or my friendships (although I was never a child who had lots of friends anyway).

From the beginning, my family has not only supported

(Author's personal collection)

my dream of acting, but they've also kept me grounded along the way. They've always made sure I've stayed humble—never letting my ego soar out of control, no matter how well my career might be going, and never allowing me to feel crushed by the devastating lows that are almost an inevitable part of being an actor.

Of course, I've seen other parents driven by motives of their own. I grew up with kids who were literally supporting their families with their acting paycheck. Pretty sad. If that's why a kid is acting—if it's the parents' dream and not the child's—it's not going to work. In my own childhood, I loved every minute of auditioning and acting. But it can be a pretty terrible life when it's not the life you want.

So how do I respond when parents approach me and

ask, "How can I get my kid into acting?" When parents seek my advice, I tell them, "If your child really wants to give it a shot, go ahead and see if she likes it. But if she doesn't, you've got to follow her lead and let her back off. If she starts to complain about not getting to see her friends or if she's falling behind in her schoolwork, then it's time to reevaluate."

Bitten by the Acting Bug

It's almost a joke, but it's true: No matter what your age, if there's anything else in the world besides acting that you could see yourself doing, perhaps you should consider doing it, or at least having it at the ready as a safety net. Breaking into the acting business is *very* difficult, and the chances of making a living at it are so slim (the city of L.A. wouldn't have any waiters were it not for all of the out-of-work actors!). On the other hand, if acting is in your blood (like it is in mine), and you just can't do anything else, then I encourage you to

(Author's personal collection)

chase your dream. I completely understand when young people (and adults) tell me that acting is something they *have* to do.

Of course, the acting business can knock the wind out of you without any warning at all. Sometimes, you leave an audition convinced that you did a great job, only to learn that you didn't get the part because they wanted a red-headed kid instead of a blonde, or they were looking for someone taller or shorter than you. They might have been seeking an actor with freckles, or someone without them. It's also possible that your acting performance just didn't impress them, and if that's the case, brace yourself. Casting directors can be brutally honest. They might tell your agent or manager everything they didn't like about your audition, with the hope that it will help you do better next time. Maybe so, but it can be tough to hear criticism, particularly when you're a kid. If you're making acting a career, however, you have to be able to hear the negative comments, and find something constructive in them.

Believe me, I've weathered my share of audition disappointments. Of course, I've also been very fortunate to land some great parts (think Sami Brady!). But during those times when I'd crash and burn at an audition, it was nice to have someone nearby to help lift my spirits. Enter my mom. She was always great, even when someone else got the part. Not long ago, she told me that when I was a kid, she'd be so disappointed for me, but all she ever said was, "Honey, they don't know what they're missing out on." She'd find a way to make me feel good about myself.

I know that 98 times out of 100, even the most talented actors are rejected for roles. But if you have a passion for acting, you learn to persevere, confident that successes are on the horizon. You learn to accept the disappointments because they're part of the business. If you beat yourself up over them, it's harder than ever to bounce back. I've gotten down on myself from time to time when I *really* wanted a part, felt I was absolutely perfect for it—but just didn't get it. I give myself a day or so to be truly bummed about it, but then I try to move on. There will be another audition. There will be another wonderful part. And I can hardly wait to give it my best shot next time.

Of course, particularly when I was younger, there was something else I had going for me in terms of self-preservation. As I've mentioned, I loved auditioning, as though it really didn't matter whether or not I got the part. I loved meeting new people. I loved getting all dressed up. Of course, it also didn't hurt that I'd occasionally get to leave school early for an audition. And I absolutely enjoyed spending time with my mom. There's a lot of "waiting around" at auditions before your name is called, and although I'd usually go over my lines a few times, my mom and I used to spend much more time just chatting and playing word games to occupy ourselves. Some of my best memories are playing Hangman or other games with my mom.

What was my favorite game? My mom or I would start making up a story, and then we'd take turns jumping in and creating the next sentence of the story line. One time, however, when I was about nine years old, I was sipping on a milkshake as we played the game. Big mistake. At one point, the story got so absolutely funny that laughter got the better of me. What happened next? I accidentally spit up my milkshake all over my clothes. What a mess!

Rather than panicking, my mom and I took action. Get

this: We splattered the rest of the milkshake all over my outfit, hoping it would look like it was part of the attire! It's not as crazy as it sounds—the part was for a tomboyish little girl, so I'd worn overalls with splattered paint on them. The chocolate ice cream fit right into the look! Even so, it was a wardrobe department's worst nightmare! Never let it be said that we didn't know how to impress a casting director!

Even during moments like this, I rarely felt any stress associated with the auditioning experience, although some of the other kids clearly were dealing with the pressure (especially those whose moms insisted that they "don't talk to the other kids; just practice your lines!"). I enjoyed performing for the adults I was auditioning for, making them smile and, if I was lucky, even making them laugh. Most of my memories are positive. I don't ever remember reflecting back on the day and saying, "Well, that was another job I didn't get!" I looked at it more like, "I had so much fun today."

Again, I have my parents to thank for the emotional smooth ride during much of my acting career. Few things irritated or stressed me out, even when I was juggling a heavy schedule at school along with the life of a working actress. From an early age, my mom and dad taught me that when there are challenges in front of me, I should not look at them as titanic in size and virtually insurmountable, but rather should break them down into smaller goals that can be achieved, one at a time. If you look only at the big picture, it may overwhelm you. But if you take it apart and confront it a step at a time, you can beat it, and not let it defeat you.

Life on the Stage and Screen

As valuable as commercials were in my own development as an actress, my appearances on TV shows, in motion pictures and on the stage may have been even more important learning experiences. In 1985, I got my first real acting job in a TV show. It was an episode of *St. Elsewhere*, titled "Santa Claus is Dead." In the show, Santa collapses at a children's party and is rushed to St. Elsewhere (where else?). It was a touching story, and I played a character named Chrissy, one of several children who arrive at the hospital, clamoring to find out about Santa's well-being as the doctors work to keep him alive. It was a small part, but I did have a few lines (although nothing was more challenging than "Where's Santa Claus?"). But, hey, I was only five years old, and it was a good stepping stone in an acting career.

I had bigger parts on other television shows, and at times the episodes dealt with very sensitive and important issues. You probably remember *Webster*, the TV series starring Emmanuel Lewis, Alex Karras, and Susan Clark (like me, Emmanuel started his career doing commercials, including some national spots for Burger King). In January 1985, when I was eight years old, in an episode called "The Uh-Oh Feeling," I played a student (named Beth) in Webster's classroom who was being molested by a substitute teacher. Webster overhears a conversation in which the teacher asks me to stay after class.

Beth tells the teacher, "I don't like it when you touch me there."

The teacher responds, "Just don't tell anybody. You'll start to like it."

It was pretty chilling and ahead of its time. It still makes me feel a little creepy just thinking about how terrible that can be for a little kid. It was the first time that a situation comedy—or just about any other TV show, for that matter—had confronted the issue of child molestation.

The program had an enormous impact. Near the end of the episode, a teacher tells the children, "If anything makes you uncomfortable, tell the principal or another adult you trust." After the show aired, kids in all parts of the country came forward and, for the first time, told what had happened to them. That's the power of television. Looking back, I'm so proud that I was part of that show.

By the way, I recently ran into Steve Sunshine, the executive producer and head writer of *Webster*. He is a producer for a daily entertainment show, and he remembers that episode of *Webster* well. He told me how proud he still is of that story and the impact it had. Nineteen years later, it's still rewarding to hear such nice things from your boss!

Along the way, I also performed in two equity-waiver plays in the Los Angeles area. I had known that I wanted to be an actress since I was a little child, and so I went on auditions for everything. My mom thought, "Why not try theater, too?"—after all, my acting classes often took on the format of performing in front of a dozen or so other child actors, which gave me a sense of what performing before a live audience was like.

At the age of six, I was cast in *The Wedding Band*. I played the part of the daughter in a very poor family who was building a porch onto their house. I had only a couple lines in the play; I remember one line, said in a very bratty voice, was: "My new tennis porch!" (don't ask me why, it's been so long I've forgotten the storyline!). It was a line that has taken on a life of its own in my real family; my dad and brothers still sometimes tease me—whenever they think I'm being bratty, I hear: "My new tennis porch!"

At age ten, I performed in another play, *The Traveling Lady*, by Horton Foote (one of America's leading dramatists). I enjoyed doing the play so much, although there was one embarrassing incident that happened after a few months of that show's run. At one point in the play, the actress who played my mom called my character's name, which was my cue to come onstage. But one night, I was backstage in my dressing room not paying attention, and I missed my cue—really missed it! My onstage mom called my name again and again for about forty-five seconds, and I was nowhere to be seen. It must have been an unbearable amount of time for her to be standing there, alone on the stage, waiting for her distracted cast-mate to appear.

Finally and mercifully, I did hear her, and I raced onto the stage. We continued the scene, rather awkwardly as I recall, and then the script called for us to exit down the theater aisle and through the audience. When we reached the lobby, I got such a tongue-lashing from her (which I certainly deserved!). She leaned into my face, shook her finger at me, and said, "Don't you ever miss a cue again! I know you were goofing off backstage. From now on, you better pay attention!"

Well, I almost started to cry. But I did get the message: Acting is serious business, and you better take your commitment to heart because everyone else in the cast is depending on you and your performance.

Despite moments like that, both of those childhood plays were so much fun and were such great experiences. Perhaps more important, they were pivotal in contributing to my growth as an actress, even at such a young age. More than ever, they convinced me that acting was something I wanted to keep doing.

I also learned that live theater is completely different than acting before the TV cameras. Even though you're saying the same lines in a play, performance after performance, something completely different can happen every night, and it often has to do with the audience. When you go to the theater, remember that you're part of the experience, not just a witness to it. The actors are definitely affected by you, whether you're laughing, crying, feeling tense, or having the time of your life. It can be such an exciting experience for the actors.

Staying Centered

There are all kinds of perks that come with acting, and when you're a kid, even the smallest ones seem pretty spectacular. When I was ten years old, I was chosen as a regular cast member of a new ABC situation comedy called *Family Man*. It starred Richard Libertini and Mimi Kennedy, and I played Mimi's daughter, Rosie. (I was starstruck meeting Richard for the first time—he's in one of my all-time favorite comedies, *All of Me*, with Steve Martin.) In one episode of *Family Man*, the script called for me to get my ears pierced. What a thrill! After all, my mom had established some age boundaries for ear piercing and most other childhood milestones, and I knew not to expect

(Author's personal collection)

Backstage on the set of *Family Man*

to get my ears pierced until I was twelve. So when I saw
the script, was I ever excited! My mom was hesitant, of
course, but she finally gave in. I got my ears pierced two
years ahead of schedule (although the pain associated with
the procedure certainly got my attention!). *Family Man*
didn't last long—it was canceled after only seven episodes—
but at least I had a few pairs of earrings to show for it.

My mom occasionally bent on other issues, but she held
her ground on many more. She was a Stage Mom in the
best possible sense; she guarded me and looked after me
without being intimidated by anyone, and she always

(Author's personal collection)

One episode of the show was about my character getting an embarrassing haircut and being teased at school. My mom was able to talk the producers into a wash-out perm. Equally embarrassing, but not quite as long-lasting.

spoke up if she thought a script crossed the line. Remember, my mom insisted that I have as normal a childhood as possible, and in an era when kids were being cast in horror movies like *Poltergeist,* she kept me away from auditions for those kinds of films.

I remember one motion picture, *The Price of Life,* which I appeared in at age twelve. It had a futuristic plot in which I played a rebellious girl named Alice, who had a tough attitude and made the wrong turn at every point in life. The script called for me to smoke and curse, which definitely didn't find a warm place in my mother's heart. In particular, she is very antismoking, and when it came to a twelve-year-old—particularly her own twelve-year-old daughter—smoking in a movie was simply out of the question.

My mom dug in her heels with the director of the movie. She was determined to reach some kind of compromise that would keep a lit cigarette out of my mouth—and she ultimately succeeded. They finally agreed that I would be allowed to hold the cigarette and pretend to smoke it. But I never really took a puff.

It was just one of several incidents where my mother intervened, speaking on my behalf, usually without me even knowing about it. She insisted that I always show up on the set prepared, take the job seriously, and know my lines. But she protected me from the tough negotiations that sometimes went on behind the scenes. She wanted me to enjoy the acting experience as much as possible without stressing out about some of the details and the fine print.

My mom also did something else that was very important: As I continued to act and was cast in better and better parts, she made sure that I stayed humble. As I mentioned earlier, Hollywood is renowned for egos soaring out of control, but my parents wouldn't stand for it. In 1989, a year after *The Price of Life*, I landed a role in a new NBC situation comedy called *A Brand New Life*.

In the show, Don Murray portrayed a millionaire father of three who marries a blue-collar waitress (played by Barbara Eden) with three children of her own (no, we weren't the Brady Bunch, despite the obvious similarities). Don's character raised his children in a permissive, free-spirited household, and Barbara's family grew up in a much

(Author's personal collection)

On location with the cast of *A Brand New Life*

more conservative environment. Much of the series' conflict grew out of the attempts to merge the families (the original name of the show was *Blended Family*, although that title never got out of the starting gate). I played Barbara's daughter, and Jenny Garth (pre-*Beverly Hills 90210*) was cast as one of my siblings.

One day backstage on *A Brand New Life*, a hairdresser was brushing my hair, and when I felt she was tugging on it too hard, I raised my voice and complained to her. Bad move.

Later, the hairdresser took my mom aside, and said, "You may want to talk to your daughter and tell her to get her act together. My job is to make her look good. If she's going to go anywhere in this business, she needs to treat everyone here with respect."

Ouch. That really pressed my mom's buttons, and she wasn't happy with me at all (and understandably so).

"Look, Ali," she told me, "you aren't entitled to a 'star attitude' here. You aren't going to be a 'star brat'—you're my daughter, you're a normal kid, and you're very lucky to be working here. So start treating people with respect, or you're not going to be here for long."

True story.

My mom was right. And I'll never forget it. Let's face it: At age twelve, it's a rather make-believe life to be on television, have people tell you how special you are, and pamper you endlessly by tending to your hair and makeup. If you're not careful, it really can go to your head. But I was lucky to have parents who would bring me down a notch or two if necessary, and make sure I kept things in perspective. It was an important lesson, and as I matured, I've never allowed myself to think I'm somehow better or different than other people just because of the type of work I do—because I know I'm not.

Nowadays, my husband, Dave, also helps me stay grounded. He's not only a wonderful guy, but it's such a relief to spend so much time with someone *not* in show business (Dave's career is in law enforcement). He's not starstruck. He's not particularly impressed with what's going on in Hollywood. Our life together really is separate from my job, and I've learned that it's important for me to avoid immersing myself in show business twenty-four hours a day. As much as I love the entertainment industry, I also know it's good for me to go home at night and enjoy time with my husband, play with the dogs, and lead a completely normal, nonshow-business life.

You Gotta Have Friends

Both before and during *Days*, I've had the opportunity to work with some wonderful people both in front of and behind the camera, and I've learned so much from them. In 1991, I appeared in *The End of Innocence*, a feature film in which Dyan Cannon not only starred, but served as director and screenwriter. It was a movie about the challenges of growing up female, and I played Dyan's character, Stephanie, as a preteenager (the late Rebecca Schaeffer was cast as the same character at a little older age). Dyan is not only a talented actress in her own right, but she was a wonderful director to work with—never pushing me in ways that would raise my anxiety levels off the charts, but still challenging me at every turn. She'd say things like, "I know you can do this. You're the best. That's why I hired you, Ali." When she'd talk to me like that, I'd think, "I *can* do this." With her support, I did.

I landed a number of other roles in my pre-*Days* career, including guesting on TV shows like *Simon & Simon*, *Tales from the Darkside*, and *I Married Dora*. *Tales from the Darkside*, was such a dark show, similar to *The Twilight Zone*. In the episode I was in, my character would say "goodbye" to people and then they would die. A pretty creepy script. I remember my mom talking to the schoolteacher on the set about all the special effects that would be required to fulfill the writer's vision. One scene required me to stand in the set while the crew filled the room with smoke. My mom was really concerned about me inhaling all that smoke, as was the on-set school teacher (who was also a social worker and was responsible to help protect minors). Fortunately, this particular production company was very responsible and didn't question the teacher's authority. A special kind of smoke was used that isn't damaging to the lungs, and the camera angles were changed to minimize the smoke that was required. The scene was still powerful, and the show was a success.

Since joining *Days,* one of my most memorable guest appearances, and one that fans often ask me about, was my appearance on *Friends* in 2000, in which I portrayed an award-winning, diva actress on *Days of Our Lives* (of all soaps!).

On the set of this successful prime time series, I could see that the cast and crew were so dedicated to creating the best possible show. Similar to *Days, Friends* has a confident cast and crew who had created a routine that was professional yet comfortable and easygoing. The atmosphere at *Friends* is different than that of a first-year sitcom that's just getting started and trying to prove itself. On the new shows, life can be hectic and even a bit chaotic as the cast and writers try to prove their worth to the network. It can be a high-tension, high-wire act with a lot of jobs on the line. However, on *Friends,* there was no tension—just a great time.

On the show, my character was a bit of a bitch, but really fun to play! I had a scene with Jennifer Aniston and Matt LeBlanc. During my first day on the set, we rehearsed the entire script. It was the first time I had met Jennifer, and she asked me, "Do you work with my dad?" (Her father, John Aniston, has been on *Days* for many years.) I told her, "Yes, in fact, we play bitter enemies. He's tried to kill me several times on the show!" Both of us laughed until we got back to the serious business of rehearsing.

On Friday of that week, we rehearsed the show again until the director and producers were completely happy with everything and ready to put the show on tape. The actual taping took place on Friday night.

Friends is taped before a live audience, a setting that was mostly new and enjoyable for me, but also the source of anxiety. After all, you're not only trying to be funny, but with an audience, you know right away whether you've succeeded. As an actor, you definitely feel a powerful energy from the audience, and since they're on your side, it's an energy that can drive you to perform even better. At the same time, even though I had been on *Days* for many years, it was a little jarring when I realized that a live audience would be out there, watching my every move. It had been so long since I had performed in front of an audience, and I did have a brief moment of freaking out a little, thinking, "Oh, oh, I'm not prepared for this!"

I remember standing backstage with Matt LeBlanc, waiting to make our entrance, and I half-jokingly whispered to him, "My gosh, what do I do differently here? Got any advice?"

Matt was so nice. "You'll be fine," he said. "It's just the same as what you've always done. Just wait for the laugh."

A *Days* Debut

Now for some *Days* trivia: Do you remember what character I played before Sami on *Days*? At the age of six, I played a character named Adrienne Johnson Kiriakis as a child, portraying her in a flashback scene when she was abused by her father. The adult Adrienne was played by Judi Evans for about five years (she later moved on to *Another World*, and as is only possible on soaps, she's now *back* on *Days* playing an entirely different character, Bonnie). When Adrienne reflected back on what had happened to her as a young girl, I played her in those childhood flashback scenes. Judi and I had scenes together just recently and I reminded her of how we'd worked together before. She had no idea that little girl was me!

Judi (Bonnie) told me when she played Paulina on *Another World* she was a *Days* fan, and that Sami was one of her favorite characters! I was so flattered—but it was definitely a "mutual admiration society"; I told her that when she came back to the show, I had to remind myself that her real name was Judi—in fact, "Adrienne" (her first *Days* character) kept popping into my head!

My *Days* debut as a young Adrienne was very exciting, even though it lasted just two days. At the time, *Days* was being shot at the Sunset-Gower Studios in Hollywood, several miles from where we tape the show today. I auditioned for the part along with a roomful of other kids, and when I was fortunate enough to get the job, one of my older cousins became more excited about it than I was (geez, I was only six!). She was a huge fan of *Days*, and so as a family favor, I got members of the cast (none of whom I had heard of at the time) to sign my script for her.

When I gave my cousin the heavily autographed script, she almost died! I gotta admit, she absolutely loved it!

Chapter 4

Although I've been an actress for almost as long as I can remember, my life is probably really not much different than yours. In fact, my motivation for writing this book is to relate some of my growing-up and life experiences to my fans while also describing some of my most interesting moments as an actress in Hollywood, particularly on *Days of Our Lives.* By telling my story, I hope you may be able to better understand issues that are relevant in your own life: finding friendships in a world where too many people don't seem to care . . . coping with peer pressures when they're taking you down paths that aren't in your best interest . . . surviving in a culture that worships thinness . . . finding balance in day-to-day living when you're being pulled in a thousand different directions . . . and discovering your inner self by examining your core beliefs and values.

Yes, I've grown up and still live in the public eye, and it's not always fun. Because of the work that actors do, all of us come under the scrutiny of the media. But despite that higher visibility, I've still had to overcome the same problems and make the same adjustments that virtually every girl and every young woman has had to do. Adolescence and young adulthood do have a way of making life interesting—at times, truly amazing; at other times, downright depressing—but perhaps my reflections on my own experiences can help you find your own way through both the good and the rocky times as you discover where you fit into the world.

Making Friends Count

No matter what your age, your gender, or your place in life, I think we can agree on the following: There are few pleasures greater than spending time with friends. If you make friends easily, you're very lucky. Not everyone is so fortunate. You might even find yourself taking them for

(Author's personal collection)

granted—but that's certainly not something that I've ever done.

I went to the same school for thirteen years—a small college preparatory school in a suburb of Los Angeles. It was very academically oriented, and I spent a lot of time cracking the books. Add to that the many hours occupied by my acting career—including auditions after school, and the making of commercials, TV shows, and motion pictures—and perhaps I didn't have as much time to make friends as some of my peers did. Even so, judging by my social life at and away from school, I was never going to be Prom Queen. Far from it.

Here's the bottom line: I always felt that a lot of my classmates didn't like me. And I never really understood why. In elementary school, I didn't have lots of friends, and that isolation only eased up a little in the middle-school and high-school years. I remember being shunned by most of the girls at school, and as best I could tell, the boys weren't particularly interested, either. I was rarely invited to parties, and I spent a lot of Saturday nights at home with my family. I certainly wasn't a very good athlete (that's an understatement!), and at recess and in gym class, I was always the last kid picked for the kickball team.

You can imagine how painful that was. I'm sure a lot of you know exactly what I'm talking about or know someone who does. Like a lot of kids who often feel that they're on the outside looking in, I would have done just about anything so classmates would like me. But I was shy and had trouble fitting in and making friends. That's what happens to some kids, and for no apparent reason. I was one of them.

It can really hurt.

I remember one girl in high school—I'll call her Lucy (I'm changing her name to protect the . . . well, whatever). She was something of a "ringleader," and she tormented me throughout high school. She seemed passionate about making my life as miserable as possible. Not long ago, in an interview in *Soap Opera Digest*, I was asked if there was one person in high school who I'd like to "get back at" by "rubbing her nose" in my show-business success. Well, guess who came to mind? For all the pain she caused me, Lucy's name was flashing like a neon sign in my mind. But during the interview, I bit my tongue and thought better of naming names. I did mention that there was someone who had picked on me in high school. But I said that I had moved on, and hoped she was happy, wherever she was. Enough said.

There were some other girls who used me for target practice as well. Even when I tried to be cool, it usually seemed to backfire. I remember clearly one incident when I was in the seventh grade. The captains of the soccer squads in P.E. class were selecting their team members, and (of course) I was absolutely terrible in soccer. After everyone else had been picked, I was the last one left, standing alone in all my embarrassment. Well, lucky me, the captain (her name will be "Kim") who "got stuck" with me didn't hide how angry she was that I had ended up on her team. She apparently felt it was just fine to humiliate me, simply because I wasn't very good. I'll never forget how mean she was during our games. When I wasn't playing to her level of satisfaction (which was most of the time), she didn't even try to hide how much she resented having me on her team. Let's just say girls can be very mean at that age.

I remember talking to some classmates after school that afternoon. I really wanted to be their friend, and perhaps as a way of trying to fit in and lash out, I complained bitterly about Kim. "She's so mean!" I said. "What's her problem? This isn't the Olympic Games!" My rant continued on and on. "Why does she have to be like that? She's such a bitch!"

As I spoke, I could see that the girls I was talking to began looking over my shoulder as if someone had walked up behind me. I turned, and was face to face with Kim.

She had heard everything.

It was like a bad movie. A very bad movie. I was absolutely speechless. I wanted to die. I don't think I have ever felt so badly.

I cried all the way home, and when I told my mom what had happened, she was upset, too, *at me*. She insisted that I call Kim and apologize.

No, not that! That was the last thing I wanted to do. Just the thought of dialing Kim's phone number made me shake. But I somehow mustered the courage. I called her at home. It was one of the hardest things I've ever done.

"You hurt my feelings," I told her. "That's why I said some very mean things about you, which was wrong. I'm really, really sorry."

As you might guess, there were some awkward moments during that conversation. But Kim did accept my apology. In fact, she was quite nice about it. No, we didn't become friends. But after that phone call, at least I wasn't embarrassed to see her at school. I also realized something important: My conscience won't let me belittle or put down people. (I'll leave that kind of behavior to Sami for now!)

Boys to Men

Now what about boys? Well, I didn't have a boyfriend in high school, if that's what you want to know. I was a little overweight—not by much, but enough to make me feel self-conscious and cut my self-esteem down to size. By the time I was starting to even think about dating a boy, I was so consumed with anxiety about not feeling pretty, it was almost inconceivable to me that boys might find me attractive.

Did I ever go out in high school? Well, yes. But here's the truth: The boy was more of a friend than a boyfriend (if you get my drift). As sad as it sounds, I actually kissed a boy on TV (on *I Married Dora*) before I kissed one in real life; I think I was a sophomore in high school before my first real kiss.

In that particular episode of *I Married Dora*, my character was the "best friend" of one of the regulars on the show. A 12-year-old boy. I was the "tomboy" who had hit puberty and was becoming a girl. At the end of the episode, my character was supposed to just lean over and plant one on the boy. I remember the director going over the scene with us again and again in rehearsal. He could see how embarrassed we both were, and since this show was taped before a studio audience, he didn't want us to get messed up and forget the scene. The whole thing went off without a hitch—it was a really cute scene. Of course, how many kids invite their grandparents to witness their "first kiss"? Yup—my grandparents were sitting in the front row of the studio audience!!!

Actually, the best relationship I had with boys in high school were with a couple of guys who would jokingly steal my backpack, ask to borrow a pen, and tease me in good-natured ways. They made me feel good because they actually talked to me, which most kids in the school didn't. It never occurred to me until I was an adult that they might have actually been attracted to me, and if I had shown the least bit of interest in them, one or both might have asked me out. But I never did anything to encourage them. I just didn't get it! Yet all those uncomfortable and embarrassing moments of my childhood have been an invaluable part of my portrayal of Sami. When my mom sees Sami's dark side on *Days,* she often teases me with lines like, "Remind me never to make you angry!" On soaps, the storylines can be so farfetched that it's often hard to "relate" as an actress to what your character is going through. I have to "replace" the storyline situation with something similar in my real life that creates the same type of feeling. And every personal struggle I've ever experienced is fair game when I face a challenging scene. So, in a very real way, I owe all those kids who tortured me in school a big "thank you"!

There were some benefits of having only a few friends, male or female, in school. Here's one: I never went to the parties where the peer pressure to take drugs and alcohol was pretty intense. I spent most of those years in something of a haze of my own making—attending class, doing homework, going to auditions, and working on *Days*—but not much else. I didn't even know that the kids in my school drank and took drugs until I was a senior! I was so naïve and felt like a real outsider.

In a lot of ways, the experiences I had on *Days* and with other acting jobs were more "normal" than my experiences in real life. Remember that on one TV sitcom, I got my ears pierced at 10 years old, an age when my mom never would have let me do it in real life. I had my first kiss on TV. The same with my first dance. The first time I made love (or at least acted like I was making love!) was as Sami on *Days*. When you think about it, it's actually pretty amusing that many of my coming-of-age moments happened first on TV.

So if drugs and drinking weren't part of my real life, what kind of "adolescent rebellion" did I go through? Well, don't laugh: *TV Guide* once wrote about a transgression in my younger days when, along with some other girls, I ran up my parents' credit line at the local grocery store. Not exactly a capital offense! Of course, it didn't make my parents particularly happy, but it didn't bring the FBI to my doorstep, either.

Breaking Out

Here's the irony: I was actually very good at making friends everywhere else but at school. Go figure! I had good friends in all of my afterschool activities, particularly horseback riding. Maybe because they had no preconceived notions of me, I was able to be myself, which they seemed to like. I really connected with some of them. We'd go to horse shows. We'd have sleepovers. Normal stuff. I also made friends on the job, whether I was making commercials or on the set of *Days of Our Lives*.

But at school, it was different. Sometimes, I came home at the end of the day crying hysterically because (in my mind) no one liked me or ever would. Even after I started playing Sami on *Days*, I still struggled with my self-esteem, and felt pretty disconnected at school. On those rare occasions when kids would talk to me, I wondered if it was only because I was on TV.

So how did I overcome this lack of friends and the insecurities that accompanied it? As I grew older and felt more comfortable living in my own skin, I became more accepting of myself. As that happened, more people began to like me.

At the time, I was convinced that I was the only one who felt so lonely. But here's what I didn't know: *Most* kids feel the same way at one time or another. In fact, the most unlikely people at my high school believed they were just as friendless as I was. A few years after I graduated, I ran into a girl who I was certain was the reason they invented the word "popularity." No kidding, everyone seemed to like her. But here's what she told me: She cried every day after school because she was convinced that she had no friends. I couldn't believe it. Of course, she was wrong. A lot of kids liked her, and I would have loved to have been her friend.

Who knows? Maybe that was the case with me, too. And maybe with you as well.

Even many of the popular kids—the ones who always seem to be busy on weekends—are insecure. In fact, that may be why they sometimes behave the way they do. Maybe they're often mean because it makes them feel superior and better than anyone else (boy, are they wrong!). As a teenager, of course, it doesn't make you feel any better or any less lonely if you know your tormenter is just as unsure of herself as you are. But that's probably the case.

In a sense, acting was an escape for me from some unhappy and insecure times in my real life. The characters that I played on TV (at least until I got the part of Sami) were pretty normal—much more normal than my own real life appeared to be. Acting let me get away from the classroom and the kids I didn't feel comfortable around. It gave me the chance to pretend to lead a grownup life, and I was definitely a different person on the set than I was at school. There was something about school that brought out the shyest and most insecure parts of me. But with acting, there's no place for shyness and modesty. You have to be bold and confident and believe in yourself.

My little brother handled things much better than I did. Ryan is a classically trained and extremely talented musician. Since he was five years old, my mom would insist that he practice for an hour a day even if his friends were over at our house. His buddies would watch TV or play Nintendo until the hour was up. The amazing thing is that he was a very popular kid, maybe in part because he stood up for himself. His friends were listening to rock and rap while he was falling in love with classical music. He listened to the music he wanted to listen to, whether or not it was popular among his peers, and he really didn't seem to be concerned whether they liked him more or less because of it. In the process, he was so popular. His friends even went to his classical music concerts. I was envious of him and his strength to be the person he truly was. I was impressed—and, of course, wondered why I hadn't inherited the same friendship gene that he did.

Looking back, I wish I had been more courageous in school. I wish I had been more adventurous and had more experiences. I wish I had gone on more group dates. Instead of trying to fit in with students who apparently didn't want me as part of their group, I should have been even more aggressive in looking for activities (like horseback riding) where I could meet people and make friends. I know high school kids who worked for charities after school or on weekends. Some made lifelong friends with other volunteers at Head Start programs. I missed out on a lot because I was so shy and so insecure.

Yet I've gained this wisdom over the years: The key is to have good friends, true friends, even if you don't have very many of them. (Of course, this is what my mom always told me when I was crying after school; I didn't believe her then, but, as usual, parents know what they're talking about.) It may be enough to have just one close girlfriend you can relate to and talk to, and with whom you have things in common. You don't need busloads of friends, especially those who spend too much of their time gossiping about others and doing their share of backstabbing. You also don't need to compromise your values in an attempt to fit in, or say nasty things just to "belong."

Stay true to yourself and who you really are at your inner core. You'll be proud you took a stand and stuck to your values.

Who Am I?

As important as a few good friends can be, I've also made an effort to get a better sense of the person *I* really am. Particularly in an industry like show business, where so much of an individual's supposed "worth" is based on superficial things—e.g., their beauty, not their brains . . . their thinness, not the kind of person they are inside—it's important to recognize the trivialness of it all and not be overly influenced by it. Sure, it sounds like a cliché, but as I identify and make peace with my inner self, I've become a much happier person and deal more effectively with the problems in my life—from relationship issues to job conflicts to health concerns. As I've recognized what's really important—and what's not—I'm making better and more genuine life decisions.

Now, don't get me wrong: My career is very important to me, and so I've learned to accept (and sometimes even embrace) most aspects of show business—the good, the bad, and the ugly. But as much as I love acting, it's only one part of my life. I've learned not to take every disappointment to heart, because in this business, there can be a lot of them. I don't let the setbacks overshadow all the good things in my life, including those that have nothing to do with the television industry. I have a happy home life. I spend as much time as possible with my family and friends. I ride horses. I ski. I've taken up golf. I've learned to play racquetball and basketball. And I never stop reading.

Finding your place in the world—and discovering the activities that make you a more well-rounded, more complete person—is a lifelong journey. Along the way, take advantage of every opportunity to bring quality to your day-to-day life.

By the way, I don't think you're ever too young (or too old!) to start this process. I remember when I was applying to colleges and was initially amazed that the Ivy League schools and other prestigious colleges were looking for students who were not only academic superstars, with a 4.0 GPA or better. They also wanted their incoming freshmen to have accumulated a lengthy list of extracurricular activities—sports, clubs, school plays, and musical performance. They wanted young people who had done charity work and made other important contributions to their community. Get the picture? In short, these colleges were seeking people who were well-rounded, with broad interests, even if they didn't excel in every one of them.

I think there's something to be learned from these college-admission criteria. No matter what your stage of life, open your eyes to everything the world has to offer. You might discover new interests along the way—some serious, some recreational, and some that may become lifelong pursuits.

I really enjoy basketball, for example. I play a little—I'll talk about my participation in Jim Reynolds' Charity Basketball Games a little later—but I'm also a huge fan of the sport, attend both L.A. Lakers and Clippers games, and I'm in a "fantasy basketball league" with several of my *Days* co-stars.

Be Flexible

Each week, I get many e-mails and letters from fans seeking my advice—not only about making it as an actress, but also about achieving virtually every other goal in their lives. I tell them how I've realized many of my own dreams—by focusing on the prize, working hard, making sacrifices—and being flexible. Yes, I've learned that unforeseen events can often derail the best-laid plans, at least temporarily; whether you're an actress, a stockbroker, a stay-at-home mom, or a professional athlete, there will still be inevitable and unexpected twists and turns that can throw you offtrack. But if you're ready and willing to roll with the punches, I think you'll emerge as a stronger person.

For most of my life, I had always assumed that I'd go to college. In fact, the issue was never *whether* I'd go to college, but rather *what* college I'd choose. But then at sixteen, my life took an unexpected turn. I got this wonderful role on *Days of Our Lives*, and it changed everything and forced me to rethink my future. As I prepared to graduate from high school, I realized that college just wasn't in the cards, at least not at the time. All those college applications I filled out were really for naught. It just wasn't practical to think I could be both a full-time student and a full-time actress. There are only twenty-four hours in a day.

Yet I remember how difficult it was to let go of my dream of college, or more accurately, to put it on hold. I know what you're thinking—"What, are you crazy? Dreaming of *college* when you've got a job like *that*?!!?!" Of course, I'm proud of what I've achieved as an actress. But at the same time, my parents have always emphasized the importance of an education. I grew up with a strong belief that a degree would be one of the most important tools I could give myself. That way, no matter what happened with my acting, I'd have something to "fall back on." So while I'm certainly happy with my good fortune to spend more than ten fantastic years on *Days*, it was still hard to let go of what I had planned for my life for so long.

By the way, for a time, I actually did try to do both—show business and higher education. I actually began taking a few evening classes at UCLA. The executive producer of *Days* told me, "If you can find a way to make it work, give college a shot and we'll try to help you out with the schedule." And he did. The show's producers helped in every way they could. But it was still impossible to find time for everything.

In my second quarter at UCLA, my economics professor provided the coup de grace to my college career. One day after class, he told me, "Look, if you're ever late for class, don't bother to show up at all!" He couldn't have been more direct. At that point, I realized that I just couldn't commit myself to college right then. Sometime in the future, maybe—but not then.

I still keep my mind active. As I mentioned, I read all the time, and read all kinds of things—from magazines (*Vanity Fair*, *Entertainment Weekly*, *The New Yorker*) to every type of book imaginable, including romance novels, the classics (Jane Austin, Victor Hugo) and "chick-lit" (a la *Bridget Jones' Diary*). I frequently check out what's on the best-seller list, and I'm an easy mark for attractive displays at bookstores. I encourage others to read, too, and enjoy the challenge of taking someone who doesn't like reading and finding a book for him that he can't put down.

I was very fortunate that my own love of reading was nurtured as a kid. My aunt and uncle live in Connecticut, and growing up, I would visit them and my cousin every summer. As a preteenager, I began going to a small bookstore in their community, which was (and still is) owned by a wonderful woman named Diane, who would always recommend fabulous books for me to read. Each year, she'd ask me about the types of books I liked and what I'd been reading lately. She'd almost interview me about my reading interests. I'd leave her store with more than a dozen books that she "assigned" me to read in the next 12 months—some were light reading (fun but well-written), and others were serious fiction. I always read all of them, and when I returned the following summer, I'd give her a report on which books I liked and which I didn't.

I've been back to Diane's Books every year, and always leave with a new stack of reading. There's no bookstore like Diane's where I live, where the staff is so knowledgeable about books and that hasn't been suffocated by the warehouse bookstores.

Let me also tell you about my book group. We're all in the entertainment industry (Ari Zuker of *Days* is part of the group). Whenever all of us finish the book we've chosen to read, we meet, talk about it, and select the next book. Everyone comes with suggestions, and our new choice tends to fit into a different category than our last book—if we just finished reading a heavy or a sad story (*The Lovely Bones*, for example), we might shift to a Jane Green novel next time that's more fun and lighthearted. Sometimes we meet at one of our homes; other times, we go out to dinner and discuss the book.

I also keep current on what's going on in the world, and get most of my news on the Internet. But at least right now, college isn't right for me. And I'm at peace with that decision.

The moral to the story? You can never predict how

your life is going to unfold. I've made some tough choices, but they're choices I can live with, and I've made them with as much thought and wisdom as possible.

A Memorable Afternoon

After I had joined the cast of *Days*, most of the kids in my high-school classes knew about my acting career, and some seemed fascinated by it. Although I still wasn't winning any popularity contests at school, they'd sometimes ask me what it was like being on TV or what some of the other actors on the soap were like.

In my initial days on the show, my character Sami was being portrayed as a loving little sister and a "good girl"—before her eventual fall from grace. In one early episode, I had a scene with Carrie (played by Christie Clark), Sami's older sister, where she was teaching me how to kiss a boy. Christie began kissing her hand, while showing me how to kiss my own hand so I'd be ready for the "real thing" once a boy finally entered my life. In some ways, it was a hilarious scene—but also rather embarrassing. I remember that Christie and I felt pretty stupid shooting the scene. But our embarrassment on the set was only beginning!

Three weeks after that episode was shot, I was in my history class at school, and the teacher brought out a TV and a VCR to show us a video on World War II. Well, the videotape malfunctioned, and the teacher announced that he'd walk over to the school library to get a different video. "I'll be back in five or ten minutes," he told us.

As soon as he left the classroom, one student boldly

stood up and announced, "Hey, *Days of Our Lives* is on TV right now. Let's watch Ali!"

Oh, no. But I thought, "What are the odds that I'll be on today, right?"

Everyone cheered—everyone but me. They turned on the TV, and switched channels until they found *Days*. Within about a minute, I was on the screen. And guess what episode was airing that day? With the entire class watching, there I was, kissing my hand with as much passion as my fifteen-year-old character could muster.

So embarrassing!

While the whole class roared with laughter, I put my head in my hands, absolutely mortified. The class's hysterics continued in waves for several minutes. I wanted to disappear.

It sounds like a scene out of a sitcom, doesn't it? I wish it had been.

Chapter 5

Are you one of those people who turns on the TV set every afternoon, asking yourself, "What in the world will Sami Brady do today?"

If there's one thing you can say about Sami, she's certainly unpredictable. And let me tell you, it seems that everyone has an opinion about her. Whether you love her or hate her, you have plenty of company among the millions of *Days of Our Lives* viewers.

Can you believe some of the things Sami has done over the last ten-plus years? Her behavior is sometimes so outrageous that it's taken me a long time to get used to playing a character who provokes so much audience venom, and yet at the same time so much sympathy for the messes she gets herself into. Poor Sami. Sure, you have to admire her spunk and her commitment to what she believes in (whatever that may be at the moment!), and even her need for support and yearning to be loved. But let's admit it, there are also times when you simply want to wring her neck—as tightly as possible.

When I first joined the show in 1993, I just wasn't prepared for how crazy my character would become, and how she would evolve in so many ways—from how she behaved to how she dressed. How good is your own memory about the teenage Sami? Do you remember those Gap

(Lesley Bohm)

long-sleeved tees and vests I wore, day after day, on the show (a rather monotonous fashion statement, don't ya' think?)? And don't forget Sami's very, very long blonde hair down to the waistline that (mercifully) is a bit shorter these days (down to the middle of the back). Bryan Dattilo (who plays Lucas) teases me constantly about how I used to bee-bop around like Jan Brady, with my hair bouncing back and forth.

By the way, whenever I've cut or colored my hair, I've always consulted with the producers of *Days* in advance. A few years ago, I wanted to do something different, and decided to dye my hair red (yes, red!) just for fun. I asked the producers, and got their OK; they even said they'd write it into the script. One of them told me, "Sami's the kind of girl who'd do anything—you can count on her to throw you a curveball!" In fact, they've encouraged me to try different styles and colors with my hair, figuring that these kinds of changes will be right in sync with Sami's un- predictable character.

Looking Back

As you might know, Sami was named after her aunt, Samantha Evans (the twin sister of her mom, Marlena). If you're a longtime fan of the show, you're aware that Sami is a kindred spirit of the woman whose name she shares; Samantha was a wannabe actress who was a ruthless hell- raiser in her own right, driven by jealousy and addicted to pills. Here's just one example of her behavior: Taking sib- ling rivalry to a new level, Samantha stole Marlena's blank prescription pads (and checkbook) and drugged her sister. Then, while impersonating Marlena, she got her sister committed to Bayview Sanitarium and a series of shock treatments. (By the way, Deidre Hall's real twin sister, Andrea, played Samantha; after a few years on the show, Andrea's character was murdered by the Salem Strangler, a serial killer who preyed on women in the town—but that's a whole other story!)

As you can see, Sami Brady—as the namesake of Samantha Evans—had quite a reputation to live up to. And, of course, Sami hasn't let us down! Early on, *Soap Opera Digest* described her as a "troublemaker in training." Sami may have started out with girl-next-door goodness, but she has used her own brand of insanity to create plenty of chaos in Salem, again and again. She has fought her way through bulimia, been raped, and given birth to a baby out of wedlock. She has schemed to win the attention of one guy after another, shot one of them, and used drugs to lure another into bed. The list goes on and on.

If you're like me and find Sami absolutely fascinating, much of the credit should go to the writers of *Days*, who created and carefully crafted Sami's character from the start. Sami has had a background and a history that has helped explain the reasons and the motivation for her behavior, including how and why she evolved into the irresistible villain that she quickly became. Jim Reilly, who is back as our head writer, created the "adult Sami," based on everything that has happened to her in the past.

Along the way, I've never tired of getting into Sami's skin and seeing what makes her tick. In fact, as each new script has arrived, just reading about her antics has kept me pretty entertained! Face it, you've probably never been bored watching Sami, either.

A Little Days History

From the start, it was *Days'* unique stories and characters that attracted viewers and kept them hooked. There were some incredible and truly mind-boggling story lines that preceded Sami's emergence on the show, and paved the way for the character that I'd eventually play. Of course, there are plenty of soap operas on daytime TV that you might consider as competition for *Days of Our Lives*. But from its beginnings in 1965, *Days* was a cutting-edge soap that took risks and went in directions where others feared to tread. Unlike most soaps, which were set in big cities, *Days* called the rural Midwest its home, and America's heartland has never been the same.

Open the television history books, and you'll find that some critics singled out *Days* for assuming the lead in taking afternoon TV into the sexual revolution. According to *Time* magazine, it was the "most daring drama" on daytime television. There were story lines that dealt with sex in ways that might have left some viewers uncomfortable and squirming—but still kept them coming back for more. No exceptions. So many of the episodes were surprising, upsetting, and titillating, and people have watched by the millions. Executive producer Ken Corday once said that you're only as good as your last episode, and *Days* has always kept viewers coming back.

Over the years, there were enough affairs on *Days* to

keep most marriage counselors and divorce lawyers busy for a lifetime. There also were characters who fell in love with siblings, and mothers who dated their daughters' lovers. There were murders and manslaughters, pregnancies and malignancies, blackmail and black sheep. There were characters obsessed with greed and possessed by the devil. Some were poisoned, others merely buried alive. Yep, Salem is not a safe place to live!

Sami Finds a Home

Once Sami surfaced in that dark overcoat in 1993—supposedly after a *very* long visit with her grandparents in Colorado—there's one thing for sure: It has always been a challenge bringing her to life amid everything else that transpires in Salem. But it's a challenge that I've enjoyed and certainly tried not to let overwhelm me.

Particularly in my first few days on the set in 1993, I remember feeling absolutely astounded at times, thinking, "My God, I'm on *Days of Our Lives*! I don't believe it!" It really was a dream come true, particularly for a sixteen-year-old who loved the show long before I auditioned for it. At the same time, there was no time to be a kid. I realized that this was serious stuff. I needed to be professional, arrive on time, know my lines, and deliver them convincingly. I needed to hold my own with the amazing cast of the show. I had a pretty good work ethic before joining *Days*, but by necessity it became a way of life in no time. I was never one of those actors who was full of herself and had attitude (Thanks to my mom!), but if I had been, I realized that no one at *Days* would have ever put up with it.

In those first few weeks and months, when a scene was particularly challenging or difficult, I did sometimes ask myself, "How am I going to do this? How am I going to make it work?" Fortunately, as I've already mentioned, there were other actors on the set who I could turn to when I needed a bit of advice. Whether the script called for something subtle or something over the top, I knew that people like Deidre Hall (Marlena), Wayne Northrop (ex-Roman), and Drake Hogestyn (John) were among those who would always offer guidance if I asked for it. Making a TV show is incredibly demanding on everyone, and as actors we rely on each other to help elevate our performances to the level that the scene requires.

Another factor has been at play almost since day 1, and this probably won't surprise you: Particularly after Sami's transformation from being sweet and innocent to wicked and nasty, I've made an effort not to let her craziness affect me once the camera is shut off and the lights are dimmed. Fans often ask whether Sami's evil ways seep into my soul and actually surface in my real life from time to time. Luckily (particularly for my family and friends!), I've always been able to separate fantasy and reality. I've sometimes told reporters that Sami allows me to get any unkind thoughts out of my system. But, really, it's not something that I've ever worried about. I don't get very melodramatic on my own time, and as I hope my husband Dave would tell you, I'm usually pretty relaxed and even-tempered. You could say that I leave Sami on the set and never let her pull the strings in my personal life.

The Bulimia Story

I've already told you how Sami was introduced to America. But the first major and meaningful story line that involved my character focused on the subject of bulimia. Apparently, the writers of *Days* already had the idea of dealing with bulimia on the show before I was even cast for the part—and what a timely subject! Bulimia—the binging-and-purging syndrome that creates such chaos in the lives of so many girls and young women—is almost an epidemic in America.

Of course, as I'll write about in great detail later in the book, I've gone through periods in my life where I've been absolutely obsessed with and fixated on my weight. When the number on the scale wasn't where I thought it should be (when was it *ever* where I thought it should be?), I would absolutely freak out. It was pretty sad, but at times my happiness (or lack of it) revolved solely around my weight. It became a dominating issue in my life.

To be honest, in my more despondent moments of struggling with the scale, I thought seriously about vomiting as a way to win the battle of the bulge. More than once, I remember sitting in the bathroom at home and trying to make myself throw up. Not a pretty image, is it? But my body wouldn't let me vomit. I'd stick my fingers down my throat, but nothing would happen. I don't know—probably a mental block of some kind, my brain's self-defense mechanism, but whatever the reason, it just didn't work. Thank goodness!

But over the years, I've known a number of girls who

turned bulimia into a way of life. Some vomited after meals. Others took laxatives. I suppose they thought it worked for them, at least for a while. But I also know it must have taken a terrible toll on their health. Some bulimic girls become so ill that they can't keep any food in their stomach, even when they want to. As soon as their body senses food, they become nauseous, and vomiting becomes almost automatic. It's shocking, but that's what this culture does to so many girls who are absolutely desperate to have the "perfect body."

The producers of *Days* were really quite remarkable in the way they handled my part in the bulimia story line. On the show, the teenage Sami began binging and purging because of the difficulties she was going through in her life. At the time, I don't know whether the producers were aware of my own struggles with weight, but they certainly made sure that I was comfortable portraying a bulimic. At the time, newspapers and magazines were filled with articles about Tracy Gold, the actress on the ABC sitcom *Growing Pains*, who had gone public in 1992 about her personal struggle with self-induced starvation (anorexia nervosa) beginning at age twelve. So at *Days* and probably a lot of other shows, everyone was more sensitive than usual about the dieting obsessions and the devastating eating disorders that can occur with young actresses. They wanted to make sure that in playing a bulimic, I didn't become so immersed in my character that I lapsed into an eating disorder in real life. True story.

The producers of *Days* talked with me and my parents about the bulimic story line to be certain that we were okay with it. As it turned out, my character struggled with bulimia for most of my first summer on the show. At the time, Sami was coping with some absolutely mind-boggling stresses in her life. She dearly loved her mother and father (played by Deidre and Wayne). But things changed instantly when she saw her mom, Marlena, cheating on her father by having sex with John Black in the conference room at a publishing party. Sami absolutely melted down. She just couldn't handle it.

Then, to complicate matters (as if that were necessary!), Marlena learned she was pregnant. But things got even worse: She wasn't sure who the father was! Was it John (her lover)? Or Roman (her husband)?

Are you following this? Welcome to the crazy world of Salem!

Until that time, Sami was innocent and naïve, and believed that her parents were perfect. Of course, every kid eventually comes to the realization that her mom and dad, like all human beings, have flaws. But for the moment, Sami absolutely lost it. She became worried sick about her adored father and how he would react to the news that he might not be the father of Marlena's baby. What angst for such an insecure teenager!

As the saga played out, Sami tried to protect her father by doctoring the baby's blood-test results in the hospital computer. As a result, a very relieved Marlena believed that Roman, in fact, had fathered the baby.

Through it all, Sami continued to find herself right in the middle of this mess. And what was her way of surviving this emotional train wreck? She never told anyone that she had seen her mother and John having sex. To soothe her own pain and sorrow, she gorged on food and then vomited what she had eaten, day after day, week after week.

In Sami's mind, her family had driven her to find solace in an eating disorder, and Sami's pain was portrayed very powerfully on the show. And judging by the fan letters I received, this storyline really hit home with the viewers.

To understand this problem better, I talked with several psychotherapists at a treatment facility for eating disorders in L.A., and consulted with some private therapists as well. Looking back, I believe that we depicted bulimia in a very sensitive and accurate way, and it was definitely challenging to play.

During and immediately after the airing of the bulimia episodes, I got plenty of mail from girls who were living with anorexia and bulimia. Many of those letters were absolutely amazing. Girls poured out their hearts with very personal and moving accounts of struggling for years with eating disorders. I'm sure they cried plenty of tears when they wrote them. I shed some just reading them. They were pretty intense. In letter after letter, young women described becoming ensnared in the grip of an eating disorder, and how they had lost control of their lives. Of course, I didn't feel qualified to advise these viewers, but I was able to refer them to reputable resources for more information and for treatment, and was as understanding and sympathetic as possible in my letters to them.

Over the years, thanks to Sami and the writers of *Days*, I have felt extremely lucky to have been involved in episodes like these that have confronted very important issues in the lives of our viewers, and really touched people's lives. One of the most moving fan letters I've ever received was from a teenage viewer who described how she had followed my suggestion and gotten help. She wrote that she knew she might have to struggle with her eating disorder for the rest of her life. But her self-esteem was improving, and she felt she was finally on the right track and making progress on the road to recovery. Those kinds of letters make me realize that we're doing something important on *Days*, and I'm so proud to be part of it.

The Marlena-John-Roman-Sami story line continued for quite a while. Marlena's new baby, Belle (who, of course, was also Sami's sister), became ill, and when she needed to have blood drawn, Sami became petrified that through the baby's blood typing, her parents would discover that Belle was really John's daughter, not Roman's. So what was Sami's solution? Naturally, she pushed the envelope as far as it would stretch. She decided to kidnap the baby and sell her on the black market. That was Sami's way of keeping her parents' lives from being "ruined."

Leave it to Sami and her convoluted thinking to come up with a strategy this bizarre! It set the stage for the kind of behavior that my character would exhibit in the years ahead. The kidnapping was the first time that Sami crossed the line and committed a serious crime (if you don't count switching Belle's paternity test results because, after all, her heart was in the right place)—but, of course, it wasn't a major transgression to her. In Sami's mind, the kidnapping was something noble, trying to protect her father and preserve her parents' marriage. To her, the abduction of her baby sister was a way of rescuing everyone around her.

If you don't remember how the story line ultimately evolved (and for all you fans who have started watching since then), let me indulge you in a brief refresher course: Sami freaked out when a buyer for the baby seemed kind of sketchy, so she decided to move to Florida with Belle. Though she was only sixteen years old, Sami decided that the best course of action was to raise the infant herself. But before that scenario could ever play out, the truth finally emerged, indicating that Belle was really John's daughter. And, of course, these facts surfaced in the most shocking way possible. Just consider this: Marlena had learned the truth about the baby's real father, and shortly thereafter, she was surrounded by family members at Belle's baptism ceremony—and the secret came out right then and there! Stefano had threatened to blackmail her, and she felt she had no choice but to announce to the entire gathering that she had had an affair with someone else. It was unbelievable. Roman was absolutely devastated. Before long, he figured out that John was Belle's real father, and that all of Sami's emotional and eating problems were related to this long and bizarre turn of events. Roman left Salem, and he and Marlena divorced.

Are you following along? You practically need a road map and name tags to keep everything and everyone straight, don't you? Don't even think of trying to do a Salem Family Tree.

A Little Advice

A final interesting note: I know that viewers really relate to Sami, and they never run short of advice for her. As this kidnapping saga unfolded on TV screens across the country, mail poured in from viewers who were horrified by Sami's behavior. In Los Angeles, several people stopped me on the street and said things like, "Give the baby back! What are you doing? Return the baby."

They were so angry at Sami!

Some of my favorite letters were from fans who took the time to recount and explain the entire story line to me. One of them wrote, "Dear Alison: You need to give Belle back to Marlena immediately because the baby is very sick, and you're only sixteen years old and can't take proper care of her. Please, Alison, do it for Belle."

I respond to all my fan mail, and there's a part of me that feels like answering letters like the one above by saying, "It's only a television show!!" But I think better of it, and I'm just so grateful that viewers are so loyal and so involved that they sometimes don't seem to differentiate TV from real life!

Here's what I think about Sami and her relationship with her fans: Even if many viewers don't want to admit it, Sami does the kinds of things that they always wanted to do to their boyfriends or family members but just couldn't, because in real life people can't behave that way. That's what I love about Sami. She puts herself out there and does these unbelievably insane things. Yet as crazy as it seems, her behavior comes from a real place. It's a product of her insecurities and her love for her family. So even when she's not very likeable, fans keep coming back for more.

Good for them—and for me!

Chapter 6

If you can say anything about the fans of *Days of Our Lives*, it's that they're loyal. Many arrange and rearrange their schedules just to make sure they're near a TV when the show airs. Others set their VCRs before they leave for work or school in the morning. If they miss the show they can now surf the Internet for detailed descriptions of the day's events—the show's agonies and the ecstasies, the affairs and the afflictions, the tenderness and the torment, the passion and the persecution.

Just a typical day in Salem.

Remember the statistics that I cited in Chapter 1: In an average week, about six million Americans watch *Days of Our Lives*. That makes it one of the most popular soaps on television. Among college-age women, *Days* has ranked only behind *ER* and *Friends* as the most videotaped program in the United States. How cool is that?

Of course, producing an hour-long show five days a week is an immense undertaking. That works out to 265 episodes a year! There are no lengthy breaks. No summer hiatus. Barely a moment to catch your breath. Compare that to most prime-time shows, which produce about 22 episodes per season. One-hour primetime dramas spend seven to ten days on each episode. Sitcoms take five days to do a half-hour show. But in daytime, we can't air re-runs, so we are under constant pressure to produce one new hour of television every day! But it all gets done, and we're so proud of the finished product—and the credit should go not only to our dedicated group of wonderful actors, but also to the many talented, behind-the-scenes men and women: the producers, the directors, the writers, the crew, the makeup artists, the hair stylists . . . the list goes on and on. All of us work very hard. All of us want nothing more than to produce a finished product that fans love and that keeps them coming back for more.

That's the bottom line.

A Day in the Life

When fans tell me that they love watching *Days*, they also often ask how the show is actually put together. With five hours of new programs per week, some wonder if we just about live and sleep on the set. "When do you ever go home?" they ask. "When do you have time to think about anything else?"

Good questions.

Let me tell you, I'm very grateful for the professionalism of both our cast and crew. The set is as energetic and as animated as Grand Central Station, with a nonstop rush of adrenaline that lasts from sunup to exhaustion (I've heard it referred to as "barely controlled chaos"!). People are racing in all directions . . . the production staff, directors, writers, set designers, cameramen, stagehands, electricians, prop crew, wardrobe personnel, makeup artists, hair stylists, audio technicians, even the security guards. All of us know our respective roles in the process. All of us approach our responsibilities seriously and thoughtfully. When unforeseen problems arise, they're resolved quickly because we have no other choice. The show has to stay on schedule. Falling behind just isn't an option.

There's really no *typical* day on the set of *Days*. In Chapter 2, I briefly sketched out what the daily schedule was like when I started on the show in 1993. These days, I usually have early calls that require me to arrive at the expansive NBC lot in Burbank between 6:45 and 7:30 in the morning (the alarm clock jars me awake all too early on those days—it hurts just writing about it!). By the time the cameras roll, the cast looks beautiful (or handsome, depending), but at 6:45, some are a little disheveled, others shuffling quietly to their dressing rooms, eyes still half-shut, brains just getting in gear (that's me!). There's rarely the opportunity to "sleep in" on workdays, although occasionally I'm not called to the set until 1 P.M. or so (hooray!).

No matter what the arrival time, the actors may gulp down a cup or two of Starbucks coffee to help us greet the day. Then we have our hair and makeup done and begin working with the director to "dry block" our scenes, which (as I've written) means becoming familiar with the marks already laid down, indicating where we'll be standing, and when and where we'll be moving. (A one-hour script will have hundreds of camera shots, so there's a lot for the directors and the actors to remember; many of us make notes on the script and review them before the actual filming starts.) If an actor has questions about a scene, the director (or sometimes the stage manager) will help you sort them out. Then it's off to wardrobe, getting yourself dressed—and then making yourself comfortable (studying lines) in your dressing room until it's time to shoot your scenes.

If there's an extended period of time to kill in the dressing room—and there are definitely days where you have a *lot* of free time on your hands—I answer fan mail, or use my laptop computer to respond to e-mails or chat with fans on the Internet. It's so much fun to communicate with

From an early age, I loved curling up with a good book.

(Author's personal collection)

my fans this way! I'm always dying to know what they're thinking about the show and about Sami.

I also usually have a book with me in my dressing room to help pass the time. Or I'll watch TV. Or knit. Or I'll call friends and bother them while they're trying to get work done. Or I'll just hang out with the other actors, sometimes running through our lines together.

Some actors take a catnap. Others get a little exercise (can't sweat too much or the wardrobe and make-up departments will kill you!). Or they'll grab a late breakfast or an early lunch on the studio lot (I'll talk later about the super-low-calorie meals that so many actors seem addicted to!). There are a thousand ways to pass the time, but I try not to allow my mind to stray too far from the scenes that I'll be taping sometime that day.

Practice Makes Perfect?

Now, what about rehearsals? Well, if you're an actor who feels the need for a lot of rehearsing, maybe soaps aren't for you. Remember, there's an hour show to be taped *every day!* So because of the time pressures, extensive rehearsals (or run-throughs) are something of a luxury. We might run through a scene once—at most, twice—before shooting, often a dress rehearsal where everyone is in complete makeup and wardrobe. And you better know your lines right out of the box, because there's just no time or tolerance for someone to be stumbling through their dialogue after they've arrived on the set and shooting begins. Thinking back to when I started on the show, the limited rehearsal time was a little nerve-wracking at first, and it was really an eye-opener to be thrown into the fire with seasoned actors. Even though I always knew my lines, I'm sure my comfort level would have risen considerably if we had more time for rehearsing. But that's when I really benefited the most from advice from Deidre. It's amazing how fast I got the hang of things, thanks in large part to the support of the veteran cast members, as well as the wonderfully understanding producers and directors. I owe them a huge thank you.

These days, we might get a script a week before we shoot it, but don't kid yourself that this gives us a generous window of time to become familiar with it. Depending on how busy we are shooting previous scripts, and how much camera time we have on those days, I may not get a chance to look at the new script until the day before we tape it. To add to the pressure-cooker atmosphere, episodes aren't necessarily taped in order, so to keep the story flowing accurately in your own mind, you need to stay focused to make sure your own character is always reacting appropriately within the context of the story line, even if the filming itself is rather fragmented.

Fortunately, I can learn my lines pretty quickly. I've developed an amazing short-term memory. But there's a catch: Don't ask me about the script we shot a week or two ago; those lines have disappeared somewhere within the creases of my brain, probably never to resurface! (I sometimes joke that I wish I had had this same great short-term memory when I was in school; I could have learned just about anything for a test in nothing flat!—just as long as the exam was sometime within the next twenty-four hours or so!)

Can You Do It in One Take?

Because we're working on such a tight, unforgiving schedule with *Days*, there's also not much room for error once the "ON AIR" sign is lit and the cameras are rolling. The goal is pretty simple: Wrap up each scene in just one take (although sometimes it takes two or three). We're moving at such breakneck speeds that, at times, mistakes are made—maybe the lighting isn't quite right in the first take, so the scene is reshot. Or perhaps an actor stumbles over a line—never me of course. (Just kidding! They have a "blooper reel" at every Anniversary party, and I blush every year dreading how many of my stumbles, both verbal and physical, end up on that tape!) Inevitably, things happen that impede the race to the finish line, but you can't let too many of those glitches get in the way and interrupt the flow. It really is a high-stress atmosphere, driven by the need to get it right and get it finished. And here's the good news: We usually do.

By the way, there's really neither the time nor the inclination for much ad libbing on the show. The scripts are so carefully crafted and story line-specific that you really can't mess with them. Of course, there are occasional exceptions to the rule: Particularly in the early days when I was playing a troubled adolescent, the writers were receptive to my suggestions when the script contained teenage slang. After all, "teenspeak" seems to change almost daily, and what's cool today can be so uncool tomorrow. So I'd sometimes tell the writers, "I really don't think kids talk that way." After a while, they actually relied on me to add the "whatevers" and the "likes" where it was appropriate.

(Like, totally!!) Other times, they'd write a scene where Sami was using an expression or an idiom, and I'd have absolutely no idea what it meant! Before long, they told me, "Ali, if you're completely in the dark about this piece of dialog, then a sixteen-year-old wouldn't be saying it. What would you say instead?"

Of course, Sami is in a league of her own. She has rarely met a wicked thought or act that she didn't embrace, so she's prone to saying some pretty outrageous and embarrassing things on the show. At times, upon reading the script, my initial reaction is, "C'mon, she's not so dumb or so evil that she's going to say something like that!" Or is she? One time my executive producer said, "Ali, I'm really happy that you've identified so completely with your character and taken her side. But she's a villain! The reality is, this is the way she'd talk and behave. Don't you see it?"

He was right. I should have saved my breath! The script stayed untouched.

The heart of the matter is that while we may reshape a few lines of dialog here and there, it's rarely anything major. Obviously, neither I nor any of the other actors have the freedom to change the character's logic or the direction of the story line (as in, "Well, if you really want to know, my preference is that my character doesn't die on the operating table and disappear from the show altogether!"). But if you have trouble saying a particular line the way it's written—if it just doesn't roll off your tongue like it should—you can do a little fine-tuning without ruffling any feathers or sinking the ship.

With *Days* being an ensemble show, the writers work hard to make sure every word is perfect and every actor gets his or her share of scenes and lines. As a result, sometimes you work five days a week; other times, just a couple. You never know what to expect until you check the schedule and then adjust your personal life accordingly. Some weeks, the pace gets accelerated into fast forward, and we'll tape six episodes in five days, building in a little breathing room so we can take a couple weeks off around Christmas, for example. But other weeks, the pace is a bit slower.

So like everyone else on the show, I've learned to be flexible. You might have to adjust to last-minute script changes during the day. Or portions of particular scenes might be designated as "tentative cuts," which means they could be preempted at the time of taping without altering the story line itself. As an actor, you have to be so familiar and comfortable with the script and the scene that, at the drop of a clapboard, you can adjust to instantaneous cuts and never miss a beat. Ain't that a challenge!

As each day of shooting is laid out, you may have five scenes spread throughout the day. But if all your scenes are scheduled for morning shoots, you might be finished by 10 A.M. and be on your way home by midmorning. (I know, days like that are awesome!) On most days, though, you better be psyched up and ready for the long haul. You'll stay on the set until you're done, which might mean a "wrap" at 4 in the afternoon, 7 in the evening, or past midnight. It can be pretty grueling sometimes, and you have to pace yourself through the day (sorry, no yawning allowed during the late-night shoots—the director sometimes has to remind us, "It's a party scene . . . wake up!"). Then you have to get as much rest as you can that night in anticipation of a new (and full) day starting early the following morning!

I'll never forget one day, we were shooting a big party scene—those always take longer because the more cast members in a scene, the longer it takes to shoot. Anyway, my call time was 6:15 A.M. because they had so many people to get ready in time for the tape to roll at 9 A.M. We didn't finish those scenes until 2 A.M. the following morning(!), and my call time for the next day was 6:45 A.M. I thought about my half-hour commute to and from work, and went to my makeup artist at the time, and said, "Nina, please call me and wake me up when you're ready for me," and I slept in my dressing room that night! By the end of the second day, I ended up going two full days without going outside once. It was kind of weird. At one point I even asked, "What's the weather like out there?"

Who said showbiz was all glamour and glitz?!

A Heartbeat Away from Death

Despite the hard work, the payoff comes in fabulous letters from fans, who tell us how much they love the show and how important it is in their own lives. They'll often describe their favorite Sami story lines and ask me about mine. In this and several subsequent chapters, I'll tell you about some of my favorite *Days* scenes and story lines, and some behind-the-scenes experiences with them. (If you're caught up on your *Days* history, feel free to skip ahead to Chapter 7, or bear with me as I describe the details of several of the more intriguing plotlines. . . . Grab a pen and paper if you need to take notes!)

When I think of my own favorites, the reason they rank so high is often because they were particularly challenging for me. They pushed me as an actress, motivating me to achieve new heights and reach a new level of performance.

With that in mind, do you remember the death row story line in 1999 where Sami was on the brink of execution? And I mean *falling off* the brink!

Of course, Sami's no angel (trust me on this one!). But she also may not strike you as a hardened criminal whose photo belongs on a Post Office bulletin board. In this particular story line, however, she did end up convicted of murder and sentenced to death. Her downfall began with an ugly custody fight with Lucas (played by Bryan Dattilo), the father of her child. But, of course, there was a lot more going on in Sami's life as well, including her obsession with Austin and her lifetime chase after him. As if that weren't enough, enter Franco Kelly (played by Victor Alfieri). Sami was at a particularly vulnerable place in her life, and Franco decided to exploit it. He saw Sami as his ticket to a green card that would allow him to stay in the country and avoid a contract on his life by a Mafia family in Italy, and he promised to help Sami drive a wedge between Austin and Carrie. (Stay with me here . . .) He also started to seduce Sami, and she began to fall madly in love with him. Before long, and to save his own skin, Franco proposed marriage—and (leave it to Sami!) she jumped at the offer. Sami was clueless, and she convinced herself that with Franco, she could finally end her preoccupation with Austin. So she answered "yes" to Franco faster than you cay say "You've got to be kidding, Sami!"

Let me digress a moment and tell you about one of the more unforgettable moments in this Franco storyline. At one point, when Sami thought that Franco was cheating on her, she struck him on the head and knocked him out in the Titan building complex, then stripped him of his shirt, wrote "DOG" in red lipstick, and pushed him out onto a window washer's platform. When Franco regained consciousness, he began begging for Sami's forgiveness from the sky-high platform. With Sami peering out at him from a window, he desperately tried to sweet-talk his way back into her good graces, hoping to convince her that he had actually been loyal to her. At one point, he pulled Sami's head forward to kiss her—and accidentally banged her (aka" my") forehead into a post on the window.

Ouch!

My head practically bounced off the window pane, and the cracking noise must have nearly shattered an eardrum or two of the sound man! It was another klutzy Sami moment—and I can tell you that there have been quite a few over the years. We had to reshoot that scene with stars still spinning around my head!

Before the passion could be cooled down a bit on Sami's love affair with Franco (and before the forehead bruises could completely heal), events began spinning out of control. Other Salemites had a much clearer vision of Franco's real motives, and at one point, as Kate was on the brink of exposing him to the INS, Franco started to attack her, and Lucas grabbed a gun and killed Franco.

What a mess!

As you've probably guessed—(this is *Days of Our Lives*, after all)—the story didn't end there . . . not by a long shot. Austin had confronted Sami on her wedding day with proof that Franco had been cheating on her. Enraged, Sami had stormed off to confront Franco, screaming "I'm going to kill him!" But she was too late! She walked in and saw Franco's dead body, and fainted . . . and that gave Kate an absolutely malicious brainstorm. She hurriedly wiped the murder weapon to remove Lucas's fingerprints, and placed the gun right in Sami's hand.

As some of you may remember, when Sami woke up she didn't remember a thing about what had happened. But there was the murder weapon cradled in her hand, and Franco was lying dead next to her. Could she have really killed him?

Almost immediately, the wheels of "justice" began turning, and Sami was the prime target. In all her insecurity, Sami wondered if she might have actually pulled the trigger and murdered her fiancé ("Maybe I really did do it," she said). But she just didn't know. She couldn't remember.

In seemingly no time, Sami was indicted and went on trial. But her memory gradually began to return, and during a Christmas Eve church service, she started having flashbacks and memories of seeing Franco upon his demise, and she finally pieced it all together. She vividly recalled walking in and seeing Franco already dead on the floor. In the middle of the church service, she suddenly yelled out, "I didn't do it!!" It was her Christmas miracle.

Maybe Sami had realized that she was innocent, but no one believed her. After all, she had lied so many times about so many other things. So why would anyone believe her now?

Waiting for the verdict, Sami was a wreck. High anxiety. Tight throat. They really wouldn't convict her, would they?

When the jury finally cast its votes, Sami was convicted of murdering Franco, her fiancé. Her sentence: Death by lethal injection.

Sami, stunned and distraught, was transported to death

row and waited for the inevitable. But she also decided that she wasn't about to die without a fight—and not a run-of-the-mill fight at that. Crushed when Lucas married someone else (it was Nicole) to get custody of their son, Sami's scheming shifted into overdrive. She pretended to collapse from an anxiety attack and was rushed to the hospital. Then, in typical Sami style, she poisoned the guard assigned to watch her (not fatally) and escaped from the hospital. In no time at all, she had snatched her son Will and crossed the border into Canada, along with perhaps the only person who believed she was innocent—Austin.

Still paying attention? If your brain is overloading, please feel free to take a break and regroup!

Okay—so, Roman tracked down Sami in Canada, and convinced (well, forced) her to return to Salem and fight to clear her name. She finally agreed, but as soon as she was back in custody, the district attorney persuaded the court to have her executed immediately. (Yeah, *thanks*, Dad!)

The story continued to build (it took more than a year for the entire saga to be presented on *Days*). Audiences across America were tied in knots and became glued to their TV sets. VCRs were working overtime. Would Sami somehow escape her ominous fate? Or would she finally die (and in the process, exile me to the Hollywood unemployment line!)?

As the clock ticked, Sami's demise seemed like a dead certainty (no pun intended!). But as her despair deepened, events continued to unfold in an even more bizarre fashion. Kate became worried when Franco's friend threatened to reveal incriminating information, and she panicked. Kate's solution: She gave the hapless friend an injection of saline, and he lapsed into a coma.

Sami's crunch time finally arrived. Just before the stroke of midnight, she was led to the death chamber, and was strapped down with her arms stretched out to her sides in a Christ-like pose. She was in tears, hysterical, anticipating the worst.

But wait a minute.

Before I tell you how it all ended, let me tell you about how challenging it was to play Sami as her execution approached. There were schmaltzy but very demanding scenes where Sami said a tearful goodbye to her son and the rest of her family. What agony! All the while, as Sami stared death in the face, she finally realized how selfishly she had behaved for so many years, and how her anger and bitterness had created upheaval in the lives of so many of the people around her. With death looming, she and her mother, Marlena, finally reconciled. After so many years of being go-for-the-jugular enemies, Marlena cradled Sami in her arms within the prison walls. Sami suddenly seemed so fragile. Marlena sang her a lullaby. Both of them wept. Both were able to forgive the other and forgive themselves. And Sami grew up a little—but perhaps too late.

I'll never forget those scenes with Deidre. They were high-stakes, highly emotional scenes, beautifully written and wonderfully directed, and Deidre was absolutely amazing. I had to draw from deep within to reach the emotional intensity that the script called for, and I'm so proud of those episodes and how moving they were for millions of viewers.

To make the execution scene itself even more challenging, here's something that most people don't know: I'm very claustrophobic in real life, and being in that make-believe death chamber, strapped down on the execution table and pleading for freedom, it was actually extremely

(Author's personal collection)

Sami in happier times with mom, Marlena, and her twin, Eric.

traumatic—both for me and for Sami! Yes, I knew that these events weren't happening in real life, but let me tell you, there were moments where I absolutely experienced every ounce of terror that Sami was feeling. I felt truly threatened. I was petrified. Real tears streamed down my face as the fatal drugs were injected into my veins.

As a side note, while I lay on the execution table, filming this incredibly dramatic scene, the crew took a five-minute break. Shooting temporarily stopped, and the director asked if I would mind just staying there, strapped down, until filming resumed. Well, claustrophobic or not, I agreed because it was so much work for the prop department to strap me back in. But it was traumatic to lie there with my arms and legs restrained, unable to move at all (not even to scratch an itch!). Bobby Bateman, one of the prop guys, brought me a glass of water with a straw, and held it while I took a sip. Then, sure enough, about that time my nose started to itch. Can you imagine what it's like to have to ask someone to scratch your nose?

Well, if you're a true Sami fan and just can't get your fill of her wild and weird world, you probably remember the end to the execution story. Just as Sami was given the lethal injection, Lucas burst into the room (he had decided to give himself up to save Sami, and spent the whole episode trying to get there in time to stop the execution), and he confessed that he had murdered Franco. At that moment, the governor placed an urgent call and the execution was halted. Sami was saved—or was she? The deadly poisons were already moving through her veins. In an instant, she slipped into cardiac arrest. She was rushed to the hospital and nearly died. That's right, *nearly.*

Of course, Sami did survive (both my agent and I are forever grateful!). She had a memorable reunion with Austin, and her obsession with him was resuscitated at about the same time that she was. Not long thereafter, she bumped into the Salem district attorney who had prosecuted her for the murder, who told her, "I'm really sorry about the whole execution thing; would you like to go out sometime?" Or words to that effect.

Can you believe it?!

Well, dear readers, that was my own near-death experience. While I could tell you that Sami and everyone else lived happily ever after, I think you know better. C'mon, this is Sami we're talking about!

Chapter 7

Almost from the beginning, I learned just how important *Days of Our Lives* is to millions of Americans. And maybe their devotion to the show isn't that surprising.

Just think of it this way: *Days* comes into your home for an hour a day, five days a week. If you're a loyal viewer, my fellow actors and I probably spend more time with you than anyone but your closest family members and friends. So like part of the family, when our characters have one of those "I-can't-believe-she-did-that" moments—saying something that you find absolutely crazy, or acting in ways that border on the absurd—you'll probably let us know.

Fans usually write very positive letters, but I also get some correspondence from viewers who tell me quite bluntly how unhappy they are with the way my character behaves. "How could you do that?!" they ask. "What were you thinking?!" (The thing is, I'm not the master of Sami's fate—I'll leave that to *Days*' writers.) Fans write detailed letters that describe how they handled situations in their own lives, and seem baffled that Sami could have managed the same circumstances so poorly. In the process, they sometimes reveal secrets about their personal lives that they may have never shared with anyone else (except perhaps a psychiatrist here and there, and maybe Dr. Phil!). On occasion, they even ask me for advice on how to regain custody of a child after a divorce, or how to make peace with their mom. They see Sami on TV every day, and if they don't have anyone else in their life who they can trust, they sometimes turn to me.

The same goes for our hairstyles and our clothing on the show. If our physical appearance sends chills down their spine, we might hear from them about those issues. No problem! I love to hear what you're thinking. Through letters and e-mails (and in the very active *Days* online message boards), fans often try to set us straight, and I'm so happy that viewers feel comfortable letting us know what's on their mind, whether their comments are positive or negative. My favorites are the fans who pick apart each moment in a scene, analyzing and overanalyzing every expression, trying to figure out what the character was thinking and/or feeling. It only shows that *Days* means a lot to them; they feel a certain ownership of the show, and they want to be "part of the action." These fans just can't get their fill, and they're very opinionated about how they want the story lines to unfold and the characters to behave. And I think that's awesome!

Can't Get Enough of Days!

At times, I'm actually amazed when fans tell me how dedicated they are to the show. Nothing, it seems, gets in the

(Lesley Bohm)

Getting ready for
one of my first photo
shoots

way of their watching *Days* and following their favorite story lines. If you think the Postal Service is committed to delivering the mail through rain, sleet, and snow, *Days'* fans go the same extra mile to make sure they don't miss even one line of dialogue or a single misdeed or sinful act. Some take later or extra long lunch breaks at work to make sure that they're in the employee lounge when the *Days* hourglass appears on the screen. They'll interrupt a shopping spree and rush to a row of televisions at an electronics or department store. They'll watch in their cars on a TV plugged into their cigarette lighter. They'll spend hours trying to make sense of the owner's manual for their VCR, just to make certain that they properly record the show each day.

Some college students tell me that they select their courses each semester with *Days* in mind, making sure that their classes don't conflict with their soap viewing. When I was at Harvard University a few years ago touring the campus, *Days* was playing on the television in a dormitory lunchroom, and sure enough, there was a large group of students perched around the TV set. (Even at Harvard, studying for finals can wait if Sami's getting herself in trouble!)

When a major news event preempts *Days*, watch out! My advice for the network's switchboard operators is to fasten their seat belts! They've been bombarded with angry phone calls from fans who can't seem to live without their daily fix of the romantic adventures of Bo and Hope, the passionate drama of Marlena and John, or the greedy-on-the-outside-but-secretly-dreaming-of-true-love-on-the-inside Nicole Walker. Sure, the news bulletins may be important to the news desk, but fans seem to prefer reading about the floods, fires, and wars in the morning paper rather than having them take over afternoon television. Legend has it that back in 1973, when the show was pre-empted by live coverage of the Watergate hearings in Congress, many fans went absolutely ballistic, particularly when the episodes aired revealing the fate of one of the Hortons, Mickey (played by John Clarke), after he had suffered a massive heart attack. Mickey was in real trouble. He was in critical condition and close to flatlining. He was rushed into the operating room for emergency bypass surgery, and his life teetered in the balance. Fans across the country were holding their breath and saying a prayer.

But what did viewers see as they awaited Mickey's fate? How about the latest testimony about the Watergate scandal? So many *Days* fans were seething. After all, they could find out about Nixon on the evening news. But they needed to know about Mickey *now!*

Fan Feedback

I'm so grateful for our fans and so moved by their commitment to the show. I love it when they recognize me on the street, and approach me for an autograph or just to say "hi." I don't mind sharing a few moments with them because that's part of my job. So I try to be as generous with my time as possible. Also, I secretly like each opportunity to show fans that in "real life" I'm not at all like Sami.

Sometimes the circumstances of these encounters can be pretty funny. Fans may see me on the sidewalks of L.A., and they're just not prepared for bumping into a TV actress. They don't want to let me get away, but they don't know quite what to say, either. They need a few seconds just to sort out their thoughts so they can say what's on their mind. But in the meantime, they may stammer for a few seconds, or become just totally speechless! It always brings a smile to my face.

I really think it's so cool when people just want to tell me that they like Sami—or even that they *don't* like her— and that they're having so much fun watching the show. But before I have you believing that *all* of my encounters with fans are absolutely wonderful, let me set the record straight. Sometimes, they're *not* interested in singing our praises. Fans have cornered me in restaurants or clothing boutiques, and have really let me have it when they've been so inclined. They might blurt out something like, "I watch *Days* all the time and I *hate* you so much!" Geez! ☹

On occasion, I'm really startled by a comment like that. But after the initial shock, I realize that they're talking about Sami—(at least I hope they are!!)—and they're just taking me along for the ride!

I've gotta admit that there have been some incredibly awkward situations from time to time—but in retrospect, they're usually pretty funny. Imagine being in a public restroom at a restaurant, and fans recognizing you and wanting an autograph? Picture coming out of a bathroom stall, and finding someone standing there, waiting for you, pen and paper in hand, and dying to get your autograph. Face it: That's pretty uncomfortable!

At times, fans seem to forget that I'm a normal person just like them, and that I have a life and have feelings. At the same time, I understand that fans sometimes get excited when they meet an actor who they see on TV every day, and with very rare exceptions, they aren't being intentionally inconsiderate.

I've also got to thank my husband, Dave. He is so patient when we're together in public and fans approach me. He knows it's part of being an actress, and he's very supportive. It never seems to bother him—well, almost never. I remember once when a fan was particularly rude (probably unwittingly) and Dave became really irked. It was a few years ago when we were dating, and Dave and I were at a restaurant, waiting to be seated. We were having an "intimate moment," standing no more than a foot apart from one another. There was plenty of eye contact and electricity between the two of us.

Then out of nowhere, a fan appeared. She literally stepped right between Dave and me, with her back to Dave, as if he didn't exist! Not only did she start talking to me as if Dave weren't there, but she called me a "bitch" and in a raised voice, proclaimed, "I just *hate* you!" Now, I realized almost immediately that she was just joking, telling me how she felt about Sami. But she was a bit impolite, don't you think? Not to mention that Dave took a little longer to realize it wasn't his girlfriend this woman was attacking, but rather a *character* on TV. It took Dave a while to get used to that kind of attention, but these days he's an old hand at dealing with fans. In fact, now he helps ease a fan's embarrassment and sets them at ease by offering up a pen for an autograph or suggesting that he take a photo of us together.

On other occasions, I've been out in public and really rushed, trying to get to a meeting or a doctor's appointment. In those cases, I always feel uncomfortable having to tell people, "I'd love to talk, but I really have to go." A few years ago, I remember being in such a huge hurry that I didn't even take the time to explain to a fan that I couldn't talk with her. I just headed for my car to dash to my appointment. Way to go, Ali!! Afterward, I felt just terrible. The fan seemed *so* disappointed! What would it have cost me to give her a smile and a very quick explanation of the appointment I had to get to? I really beat myself up about that one. As much as possible, I really make an effort now to give fans the time they deserve. If I only have five minutes, I'll explain why I'm in a rush, I'll take a moment to sign an autograph or take a picture, do my best to make it a positive experience for them, and then run along (in some cases, literally *run* along!).

I think I owe it to my fans to go the extra mile for them. With very rare exceptions, they've always been absolutely wonderful to me. More than 99 percent of the mail I get is from fans of *Days* who are totally supportive, and just want to reach out and tell me how they feel about the show and about Sami. I participated in an online chat not long ago, and more than 500,000 Sami-Fans logged on and took part. More than 25,000 unique new visitors access the Alison Sweeney website each week (for the uninitiated, check out *www.alisonsweeney.com*). I will never, *ever* take that fan interest and support for granted. ☺

But fans do get caught up in the story lines, and sometimes they just have to get things off their chest. Earlier in the book, I told you the story of the woman who approached me on the street during the episodes in which Sami had kidnapped her baby sister—and she swung her purse at me and yelled, "Give the baby back!" That's how emotionally involved people are in the show. To some of them, there doesn't seem to be a line between fantasy and reality.

By the way, when people stop me on the street, and tell

me that they're big fans of *Days*, I often tell them that *I'm*
a big fan of the show, too. I really am! When they describe
what they love about the show, I often find myself nodding
my head and thinking, "Me, too! I feel exactly the way
you do!" I sometimes freak out, too, when I read the upcoming scripts and find out what kinds of predicaments
the characters are getting caught up in next. It's as exciting
for me as it is for you!

Celebrating Days' Fans

I think I can say the following not only for myself, but on
behalf of every other actor on *Days*: You and all our other
fans are so important to us, and we think it's important to
show it, not just say it. That's why we hold an absolutely
awesome Fan Weekend for *Days*' aficionados in Los Angeles each spring—usually in May or June—and about 600
fans each year can't wait to participate. There's a lot of
chatter, a lot of laughter, a lot of hugs, and a lot of fun for
both the cast and the fans. It's such a blast just hanging out
with our loyal audience, in what turns into a very, very
long party! I hope you'll come to one of these fan events
sometime, and if you do, you'll not only be able to meet
and talk with us, but you're liable to see us sing and dance
for you, too! ☺

What can you expect? Well, in the last few years, the
cast has gotten together and put on a live show for the
fans, displaying talents that you never see on the TV show
itself. In 2003, we put on a performance to remember—
Kevin and Patrika's "Last Blast"—in which all of us donned

our dancing shoes and entertained the crowd (and without even one sprained ankle to show for it!). In earlier years, we staged our own version of *Moulin Rouge*, which was the brainstorm of Patrika Darbo (ex-Nancy) and Kevin Spirtas (ex-Craig). In those shows, some of us sang, some of us danced, and some did both (those of us who aren't particularly stellar in either category gave it our best shot, and sure had plenty of fun doing it!). I remember how Ari Zuker (Nicole) and I—and a few other brave *Days'* actresses—sweated and strained for weeks (it seemed like months!) to perfect two challenging dance numbers for *Moulin Rouge*. OK, as much as I love to dance, maybe I was in a little over my head, but we had such a spectacular time! The costumes were great, and Ari and I loved playing dress-up and dancing to those wonderful songs from *Moulin Rouge*.

What else do we do on Fan Weekends? There is an Official Breakfast for both the fans and the cast, some great raffles, a lot of Q & A sessions, and plenty of autograph signing and photo taking. In 2003, I took part in Lauren Koslow (Kate Roberts) and Josh Taylor's (ex-Roman Brady) Fan Breakfast, and I think everyone could see how much Lauren and I enjoy each other's company, which might come as a surprise because, on-screen, there's certainly no love lost between our characters, who always seem to have their daggers drawn whenever they're in the same story line. We joked with each other about hating the other's character, and shared with the audience how much we actually enjoy our fight scenes together. Lauren and I get along so well personally and professionally, and trust each other enough to really put our all into the catfights.

We feel as though that's the key to the success of our vicious knock-down-drag-out confrontations: our friendship. Makes sense in a weird way, right?

We usually close out the Fan Weekends with a Jim Reynolds' (ex–Abe Carver) Charity Basketball Game. Sometimes members of the *Days* cast have played against one another, or we've competed against actors from other soaps. Other times, our team has played a local high school team (usually leading to a pretty ugly loss on our part—no surprise there!).

Now, I can be ridiculously competitive on the basketball court (although let me put Shaq's mind at ease—you have nothing to worry about!). In 2003, I ended up with an unsightly bruise on my arm from a little too much physical contact on the court, and a couple years before that, I sprained my ankle in the final minutes of the game—and it hurt so much. The ankle swelled up to the size of a baseball—no, make that a softball!—and for the next few days back at work, I had to limp around on the set. It was such a pathetic sight! As I explained (in good fun) on my website in the aftermath of that "carnage," in which a bunch of us ended up falling over one another, there was plenty of debate over who was to blame for that pile of actors stacked on top of one another at center court! Justin (Melvey, ex-Colin) insisted upon his innocence (yeah, right!), but there were witnesses who claimed that he got a little carried away playing rugby rather than basketball. I think Frank Parker (Grandpa Shawn), who ended up somewhere in the pile, and I bore the brunt of the melee.

I'm pretty "smiled out" by the end of the Fan Weekend. The fans are so incredible; many fly in from across the country (and in some cases the world!). We have such a blast! We'll continue to have these weekend events for as long as our loyal viewers want them, and let me tell you, there's not the slightest sign of any waning interest. (See you there next spring!)

Throughout the year, the cast of *Days* participates in other extracurricular endeavors as well, all of them aimed at meeting and entertaining our fans. I remember a trip to South Carolina not long ago where the *Days* cast got to meet with fans and play a softball game. As I said, I'm competitive and want to win, but I hadn't picked up a bat since the seventh grade. I tried honing my "skills" by taking some last-minute batting practice before the game started, but here's the truth: It really didn't help much. Yes, I actually hit the ball during the game, but the New York Yankees didn't come calling afterward! At least we won the game! (There I go, showing my competitive side again!)

Almost the whole cast participates in these special events throughout the year. From charity walk-a-thons to mall-signings . . . we travel throughout the country signing autographs and meeting fans from all over. The guys (hunks) have the busiest personal appearance schedule— sometimes they are out of town every weekend doing events. We all have gotten pretty familiar with the airports around the U.S. from all the traveling we do. But the whole experience just reinforces how unique the relationship is between our characters and the fans. And I like to think that Sami has certainly struck a chord with the *Days* audience. After all, when fans vote you an Emmy Award for Favorite Villain, which happened to me in 2002, you know that your character really is stirring up the passions of viewers and leaving some of them seething. Fans have told me that they've actually used their TV sets for target practice, throwing any object within reach at the screen during my scenes—or firing off an obscene word or two when Sami has really infuriated them ("bitch" seems to be a particular favorite among Sami haters!!).

The chat boards can be just as amazing. When I check out the *Days* bulletin boards on America Online, for example, some fans really let loose on Sami (or as some of them call her, "Scami"). I guess they figure they're completely anonymous when they're online, and they don't hold anything back! They have their say and can be pretty cruel, that's for sure (I'm not joking about that!). But again, I realize that they're just letting off steam about my character, not about me—and I know Sami can be pretty irritating at times. So I try not to take it personally.

Because of the kind of person that Sami is—creating her own style of mayhem in Salem, year after year—I'm not surprised at the good-natured venom. (In a way, it shows that I'm doing my job well!) Sometimes, when I'm rehearsing or taping a scene in which Sami is being particularly bitchy, I'm sometimes thinking, "Man, Sami's going to get viewers screaming at their TV screens today!" It makes playing her all the more fun!

An International Following

While it's on my mind, here's something else you may find interesting about *Days* fans. I've found that when I travel overseas, the interest in *Days* seems to tag along with me. The show is an international phenomenon, not confined just to the United States.

During the Christmas holidays in 2002, James Reynolds (ex-James Carver), Matt Cedeno (ex-Brandon Walker), and I took part in a USO tour overseas, just months before the start of the war in Iraq. We flew from Kennedy Airport in New York to Madrid, and then traveled further into Europe to spend time with the troops stationed in the Mediterranean before they shipped out to the Persian Gulf. It was an amazing experience. We stayed on a military base and slept in officers' quarters (not fancy, but not bad!). It was so cool to hang out with the soldiers and sign autographs for them—and I was so proud of every one of them. We spent Christmas Day with them, and we even served them Christmas dinner. They were so appreciative—and they were also so young! I was twenty-six years old at the time, and I was older than most of them. We're so lucky to have these men and women who serve our country, and I made sure they knew how grateful Americans are for what they're doing for us.

Jim and I went on a USO tour again in 2003, with Kyle Brandt (Philip) and Eric Winter (Rex). You'll have to read about it on my website. . . . Oh, and I've got tons of photos from both tours posted on my site as well.

In traveling to other parts of the world, I've learned just how universal the appeal of the show has become. Of course, *Days* is watched by millions of people in the United States each day, and it is taped in Burbank, California, at NBC Studios. But eyes around the world watch our show, with a little help from subtitles or voice dubbing. *Days* has fans in all parts of the globe, from Paris to Rome, from Melbourne to Montreal to Jamaica. It really is quite amazing, and we have huge ratings in some of these countries. In fact, I've been recognized in the most unlikely places!

Here's a funny example. In October 2002, Dave and I

vacationed in Europe. It was a great trip, and we started with five days in Paris. It was the first time we had been to Paris and some of the sights just took our breath away. We spent almost an entire day in Versailles, where the gardens and the palace are truly stunning. We went to the Louvre and visited Notre Dame.

I haven't mentioned the Eiffel Tower yet because I've saved the best 'til last! It is so amazing to see it in person—even more magnificent than I had imagined—and when we went to the top of the Tower, the view was absolutely spectacular (What tourist could pass that up!). We even ate dinner in the Eiffel Tower.

Now the reason for this story: Dave and I were waiting in line to take the elevator up the Tower. The line was very long, and it snaked back and forth so you saw the same people again and again as you gradually moved closer to the elevator. And one by one, people started to recognize me (I wasn't wearing much makeup that day, and I would have preferred to have remained totally anonymous—it always seems to happen that way, Murphy's law or something). A couple of German tourists recognized me first. Then people from Singapore. And Frenchmen. And several Americans. Well, all of them had their cameras with them because they were visiting one of the most popular tourist attractions in the world—and a lot of them wanted their picture taken with me. That was fine with me, of course—although things did take a rather unusual twist. As the line wound back and forth, and I kept seeing the same tourists again and again, even those people who didn't have a clue who I was began asking to take a picture with me. (None of them asked, "Who are you again?" but they might have been thinking it!) They figured they'd take a picture with a celebrity—even if they had no idea how or why I might be well known. It was a little embarrassing—but pretty funny!

Now, one piece of advice: If you're going to be traveling to Paris, I don't recommend that you spend a lot of time in your hotel room, switching the television dial, looking for *Days of Our Lives*. (Even though I love *Days*, I have to acknowledge that there might be more exciting things to do if you ever get to Paris!!) But if TV happens to be your thing, you'll definitely be able to watch the show there. I did some press interviews with French magazines, so I spent a lot of time thinking and talking about *Days*. I found out that it comes on at 8:30 in the morning—and it airs without commercials. The last day we were in Paris, I watched the show in our hotel room, and there all of us were—*speaking French* (thanks to the art of dubbing). It was actually hilarious. (I even taped it on my camcorder for posterity!) In the episode I saw, there was a scene at Johnny Rocket's with Sami, Austin, Roman, and Carrie, talking in voices that weren't ours, and in a language that none of us spoke. To add to the entertainment value of the experience, French television doesn't air the most recent *Days* episodes—I saw a three-year-old show that day. Actors no longer on *Days* were in the episode. And we all looked *so* young!! Totally weird!

Chapter 8

Back to show memories: 1993–2002: Sami and Austin. Austin and Sami. Lives intertwined, for seemingly forever.

Almost from the beginning of my life on *Days*, Sami was obsessed with Austin Reed. He was her true love. She wanted desperately to have a life with him. She dreamed and schemed and was determined to have him for her own.

So who was this guy Austin? And why was Sami so pre-occupied with him?

I think answers to questions like these will help you understand Sami a little better and will certainly show you the kind of character I've been playing for all these years. You can find so much of what makes Sami tick in the enduring relationship (or obsession) she has had with this one man. So let's spend a few pages unraveling the Sami–Austin relationship, and learn something about Sami in the process, including the challenges I've encountered and the fun I've had playing her for more than ten years.

The Austin Saga Begins

If you're a longtime *Days* fan, you know that Austin (played first by Patrick Muldoon, then by Austin Peck) came from a difficult background—a divorced family and an abusive father who was hooked on drugs. Somehow, Austin emerged carrying very little emotional baggage (at least it seemed that way) when he showed up in Salem in 1992, about a year before Sami returned to town. Over the ensuing years, their lives became entangled in one intriguing plot line after another.

(OK, here we go again—more story lines. If you're already up to speed on everything you'd ever want to know about Austin and Sami, just fast forward to Chapter 9 and spare yourself the smallest details.)

Early on, from the time she was only fifteen, Sami fantasized about being a part of Austin's life. It became a fixation. It became her obsession. But almost from the start, there was a major obstacle in her way, coming from someone who also had the last name "Brady." Sami's sister, Carrie, had fallen in love with Austin, and in fact, Carrie and Austin planned to be married.

The thing is, Sami started out trying to encourage the two to be together. See, Carrie was horribly scarred when a loan shark tried to throw acid on Austin—it hit Carrie instead. She was so insecure about her scar that she tried to break up with Austin. Sami did everything she could think of to get her sister back into Austin's arms—I know what you're thinking: "*Sami?* Trying to *help?*" But, yes . . . it's true! And it worked, Carrie and Austin eventually reunited, and Sami was happy for them, though she never got over her teenage crush.

So when did it all go bad, you ask? Well, this creepy guy Alan came on the scene. He was obsessed with Carrie, and tried to kidnap and rape her on several occasions. When Austin rescued Carrie from Alan's clutches, he turned his evil attentions on Sami as a consolation prize. With no man to rescue her, Sami became a victim of Alan's obsession, and was date-raped by him. (I'll write more about this in the next chapter.)

Skipping ahead a little, Lucas finally discovered the truth about what had taken place and helped Sami tell her family what had happened to help her. Carrie was determined that Sami seek justice, even though Sami was violently opposed to airing the whole story in public. Carrie promised Sami that justice would be served and Alan would go to jail. But that's not what happened. Just as Sami had feared, Alan got off, and the end result was Sami's name (and photos) splashed on the front page of the tabloids. Humiliated, Sami held her half-sister responsible for not keeping her promise—forcing her into the spotlight and embarrassing her. That was the beginning of the end of Sami and Carrie's sisterly bond.

Don't you love how I'm telling the story lines as if these are real people? In some ways, Sami, Lucas, Austin, and Carrie are like real people to me—I don't know, maybe like in an alternate universe or something! I've been a part of Salem for so long now that sometimes I forget how outrageous some of this stuff can sound to other people. (Maybe I should talk to Dr. Phil!)

Sorry for digressing. Now back to our story: With Austin committed to Carrie, most sisters would have backed away. But did Sami? After the Alan experience, Sami decided Carrie wasn't "good enough" for Austin and decided to pursue him herself. As you know, Sami's on her own planet when it comes to dealing with love.

Maybe you remember that both Sami and Austin lived in the same apartment building on Guilford Street (I didn't know Sami lived on Guilford Street. I had to look it up!) and—forever scheming—she used every opportunity to win his attention. When her air conditioner broke down, she convinced Austin to fix it. When her plumbing needed repairs, Austin got the call. She'd call him to claim that Alan was after her again. You get the picture, she stopped at nothing.

But Austin wasn't a fool. He figured out what Sami was up to. Yet that didn't stop Sami's conniving—of course not. Her devious actions only got more creative. Sami certainly wasn't about to allow Austin to spend too much time in someone else's arms, particularly her sister's. And anyway, she simply wasn't very fond of Carrie . . . Okay, she detested her! Blood just hasn't run too deep in the Brady family, and the battle over Austin was enough to drive Sami toward behaviors that bordered on the bizarre. She wanted Austin all to herself, and she'd do whatever it took. It was all so crazy.

The Chase After Austin

Here's one thing all of us have learned during the years that I've played Sami: When she sets her mind to something, she won't let anything stand in her way. She even slipped a drug into Austin's drink at the Cheatin' Heart, and then tricked him into having sex with her at her apartment. Poor Sami, she was actually convinced that after sleeping with her once, Austin would fall in love with her. Well, that didn't happen. Just to show you how complicated things got, a heavily drugged Austin thought he was actually making love with Carrie instead (Sami even doused herself in Carrie's perfume to help lure him into bed!). Once Austin realized what had actually happened, he ran back to Carrie, and made Sami promise never to tell her sister that they had made love.

Well, Sami was devastated by this turn of events. No one was better at self-pity than Sami, and feeling that her world was collapsing around her, she fled Salem.

As for Lucas, he and Sami went way back (to 1993, to be exact), and had a rather auspicious beginning when, at a rock concert, Sami and Carrie stumbled upon Lucas getting out of bed with a rock star named Cherish. Later, Sami ran into him when he was dressed in full military-school uniform, appearing as preppy as it was possible to look. But Sami had his number from the start; she remembered him very vividly from their encounter at the rock concert.

Lucas and Sami became close friends (he also happened to be Austin's half-brother), and initially Sami saw him as a way to make Austin jealous. As great comrades, Lucas and Sami often schemed together. In fact, they worked together to break up Carrie and Austin—Lucas wanted Carrie, and Sami wanted Austin. Perfect, right? Wrong! Lucas (in his full military uniform) agreed to take Sami to a local dance, where she knew that Austin would see them together. In her own clueless imagination, she pictured him becoming furious, and demanding to have Sami for his own.

A side note: Bryan (Lucas) took me to a real school dance—which I'll discuss in more detail later.

Back to the story: In the aftermath of Sami's sexual liaison with Austin, Lucas did more than soothe her emotional pain and help her in her scheme to win the attention of Austin. While Lucas-and-Sami were plotting together, he had become a true friend and confidant of Sami's, and—you guessed it—Lucas and Sami ended up sleeping with one another. (That sure took her mind off Austin, at least for the moment!) Here's how it happened:

Sami had tried to seduce Austin before resorting to the "drugged drink" routine. When he turned her down flat, she began to beat herself up over it, telling herself that she wasn't pretty enough and that no one loved her. To console herself, she headed for a bar (at the tender age of seventeen), was turned down when she tried to order a drink, and then became the target of some heckling (and a spilled beer on her shirt), courtesy of a group of unruly guys at the bar. Sami was becoming frightened when Lucas unexpectedly appeared and came to her rescue, escorting her from the bar.

Poor Sami.

She and Lucas ended up at the Titan Photo Lab, where she put on Carrie's bowling shirt since hers was drenched with beer. And then Sami proceeded to cry a river—with Lucas as her audience—telling him how no one's ever going to love her. Lucas began to console her, saying, "I love you; you're my best friend." Well, in the ensuing minutes, they became *very* friendly—and ended up making love. It really wasn't a romantic thing (believe it or not)—it was more a show of friendship and demonstrating how close they were.

Well, guess who walked in on them? Austin showed up, saw Sami's blonde hair and a shirt with Carrie's name on it, and assumed that Carrie and Lucas had slept together.

He was mistaken, of course, but the confusion of identities couldn't have made Sami any happier! Sami became immediately revitalized, convincing herself that Austin would leave Carrie and (of course) want to be with Sami. Now, she had a chance with Austin—or at least that's what she thought. So she put the drug in his drink, fully expecting him to fall madly in love with her after realizing they'd made love.

You can almost imagine what happened next, right? Sami had become pregnant. But who was the father of the baby? Lucas? Or Austin?

Sami convinced herself that Austin had impregnated her— and she was absolutely thrilled. Still, the question lingered in Salem: Could it be Lucas's baby instead?

I'll discuss Sami's incredible pregnancy in a moment, but suffice it to say that she was quite content believing that Austin was her baby's father, and never sought any tests to prove it one way or the other. Even after the baby was born, she lived with the belief (or was it a fantasy?) that her beloved son Will was Austin's.

Now, I know what you're asking: If you didn't follow *Days* when these episodes aired, you're probably wondering whether—in the insane world of Sami—was Austin the actual father of her baby? Well, not really! Sami's world began to turn upside down when Will was two years old, and he and his stroller accidentally ended up in the river. Carrie leaped into the water and saved his life, and he ended up in the hospital (don't most kids in Salem spend time hospitalized with a serious illness or trauma?). While he was in the hospital, Sami saw the results of routine blood tests conducted on Will, and was stunned by the results. She realized that Austin was not Will's father—Lucas was.

Well, Sami was determined to perpetuate the lie. She

promised herself that no one else would ever learn who the father of her child was. No one would ever know that Austin was not the real father. Absolutely no one.

In the true tradition of soaps, however, the truth did come out on the day of Sami's wedding to Austin, no less (I'll get to that story later). Anyway, when Lucas finally learned that his night of lovemaking with Sami had produced a baby, he became furious. (Carrie gave her a solid right hook across the jaw—that's still a fan-favorite moment!—and I'll write more about that unforgettable punch later.) After all, Lucas was upset not only because he had been deprived of enjoying the first two years of his son's life, but also because Will believed that Austin was his dad. And Sami had used Austin's love for Will to drive a wedge between Austin and Carrie.

Lucas became almost crazed with anger. He couldn't contain his contempt for Sami. He became just the latest in a long string of Salemites whom Sami had manipulated and antagonized.

The 11-Month Pregnancy

Okay, let me tell you, I am exhausted from trying to keep that whole story straight in my head. And I'll admit I had to look up more than a few incidents to include all those details. But let's step back for a moment and talk about Sami's pregnancy. When we taped that story line, it turned into one of the more challenging periods of my time on *Days*. I was only 19 years old, and let me tell you, portraying a pregnant woman was unlike anything I've ever done in front of the cameras.

Let's put this into context: I do plan to have children myself some day, and I really look forward to the experience of carrying a child for nine months. Of course, on *Days* I wasn't really pregnant—I was just playing a pregnant woman on TV. So to look the part, the wardrobe department created a padded undergarment for me to wear. A *heavily* padded undergarment. It was *very* uncomfortable . . . both physically and in other ways, too.

As I've mentioned—and will discuss in much more detail later in the book—I've struggled with my own weight at various times in my life, including while I've been on *Days*. And with body image in mind, I've got to admit that it was *definitely* horrifying to see myself in the mirror with a big, padded belly. Of course, I knew that it really wasn't my own stomach that was getting bigger. But as they added more padding every few weeks, it didn't do much for my weight-conscious ego.

Every few weeks, I'd go to the wardrobe department and find that an extra pad had been added to the undergarment. Just what I needed! There were moments, particularly as I'd really become completely immersed in my character and the pregnancy, I sometimes would actually get frightened (as in: "I can't believe this is happening to me"). By the end of the "pregnancy," all I needed was a fake white beard and a red outfit, and I could have worked as a department store Santa Claus during my off-hours! I was absolutely huge! (If you're a mom, I really don't have to explain this to you, do I?)

By the way, did I mention that I may have also set a record by having the first 11-month-long pregnancy on television (or probably anywhere else, for that matter)? That's right—11 months! The actual taping of these *Days* episodes extended over an 11-month period—more than a pregnancy would last in real life, of course. But fans of the show never complained about the time discrepancy—either they were so caught up in the story line that they didn't notice, or they were so intrigued with Sami's pregnancy that they didn't want it to end. And at times it seemed like it never would!

As you can imagine, when Sami finally gave birth, she was ready for the baby to arrive (or at least I was!). But nothing is easy in Sami's life, and those delivery scenes were pretty challenging. Sami ended up being all alone in her parents' old house, in her old bedroom, when she went into labor. The phones weren't plugged in, so she couldn't reach anyone or call for help. So there she was, terribly frightened as she went through several cycles of agonizing labor pains.

Fortunately, Sami was finally discovered by Austin, and was rushed to the hospital. But her ordeal continued (and how well I still remember it!). She endured a full two episodes of additional labor in the hospital, with no end in sight. Finally, and mercifully, her obstetrician interceded and decided that an emergency C-section needed to be performed.

Amazing, isn't it? It was *so soap* to go through four episodes of absolutely agonizing labor and then have a C-section.

By the way, these "labor" scenes are always difficult to shoot. For one thing, as a 19-year-old actress, I had absolutely NO idea what real labor felt like for a woman. All I had to base my performance on was movies I'd seen. There was a make-up artist standing just offstage, ready to spritz me with water to make me "sweaty" . . . and then I was practically hyperventilating with all the heavy breathing and screaming I was doing. At the end of those days of shooting, I was exhausted and definitely wary of the whole process. Dave and I certainly want to have children some day, but hopefully my real-life experience won't be anywhere as strenuous as Sami's!

Austin at the Altar

The unusual relationship among Sami, Austin, Lucas, and Carrie just kept getting more entangled. And all the while, the role of Sami continued to be so much fun to play. Each time I'd pick up a new script, I'd be on the edge of my seat, wondering what kind of quicksand she and the others would be sinking into next. And along the way, it was such a blast to be in so many scenes with such great actors and good friends—Christie Clark (Carrie), Bryan Dattilo (Lucas), and of course Austin Peck (Austin).

Let me give you an example of how the lives of these four characters were so often intertwined. As I mentioned, Lucas had taken a liking to Carrie, and at one point he started doing some plotting of his own. He told Sami that if she would just lose a little weight, and pursue Austin more aggressively, she could drive a wedge between Carrie and Austin—clearing a path for Lucas to win Carrie's attention. (Just what I needed—someone to tell me to go on a diet! Give me a break!)

The thought of chasing after and snaring Austin sounded wonderful to Sami, of course. But as always, things didn't go according to plan—at least not the plan that Sami had in mind. In fact, before the plot could play out, Carrie and

Austin decided to get married—and Sami was absolutely beside herself. The wedding was all set for St. Luke's Roman Catholic Church—the same church where Marlena and Roman had been married a decade earlier.

If you were watching in 1995, you might remember Carrie and Austin walking down the aisle in their gorgeous, elegant wedding. The weddings on *Days* really are something to behold. (They draw a huge viewership, and they're fun for the actors, too.) The best part is, you never know if a wedding in Salem is actually going to take place—more often than not some terrible event takes place to stop the proceedings. This one, of course, was no exception. Sami had run away from home days after sleeping with Austin (and Lucas). Lucas found her barely surviving in Seattle (of all places) and brought her back to Salem just in time to have her appear at her sister's wedding. But seeing Austin marrying her next of kin was more than she could bear. So she took action, as only Sami could!

Compliments of Sami, one small unexpected glitch arose during the Carrie–Austin nuptials. Never one to refrain from creating bedlam in other people's lives, Sami chose the ceremony itself to make an announcement guaranteed to ruin even the best-laid wedding-day plans: She faked a fainting spell (a common soap pregnancy syndrome!) and when she "came to" she told the gathering that the groom (aka Austin) was the father of her baby! That's right—it happened right there during the ceremony, before the vows could be completed.

Well, it wasn't true, of course. Austin was *not* the baby's father. But who can be bothered with facts at a time like this! That wedding day would definitely be something to remember.

Sami at Her Worst

Sami's manipulations were barely beginning. Without spending the better part of this book recounting every last detail (I think I've done enough recapping already), suffice it to say that the scripts sure kept me busy with one Sami psychodrama after another. Sami worked hard to persuade Austin that he really was Will's father. Then all of their lives took a bizarre twist when the baby was kidnapped by Sami's neighbor and ended up in Europe. Ever the schemer, Sami convinced Austin that the best way to get the child home was for Sami and Austin to go through a marriage ceremony. So in Paris, Sami and Austin actually tied the knot (although if Austin had known the truth at the time, he might have decided that the knot would fit better on a noose around Sami's conniving neck!). Sami, of course, was ecstatic with this turn of events, and when Austin agreed to marry her, she finally felt she could claim the trophy that she had sought since she first set eyes on him. But as for Austin, he was much more inclined to consider his marriage to Sami as one of convenience, simply for the sake of Will and his safe return home. He didn't show much interest in consummating his marriage with Sami on their wedding night, and much to her chagrin, the marriage was eventually annulled.

Meanwhile, Carrie and Austin ultimately did get married, but somehow we knew that their legal union wouldn't last forever, nor would Sami ever accept a life without Austin. That's just not Sami's style. When I saw the next few scripts, I realized how correct I was. Marriage license or not, Sami was determined to destroy the Carrie–Austin

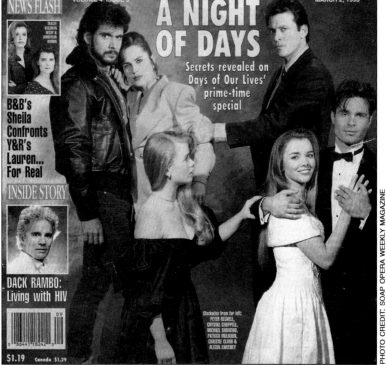

SOAP OPERA WEEKLY

NEWS FLASH

VOLUME 4 ISSUE 9

MARCH 2, 1993

TRACEY BREGMAN RECHT & KIMBERLIN BROWN

A NIGHT OF DAYS

Secrets revealed on Days of Our Lives' prime-time special

B&B's Sheila Confronts Y&R's Lauren... For Real

INSIDE STORY

DACK RAMBO: Living with HIV

Clockwise from far left:
PETER RECKELL,
CRYSTAL CHAPPELL,
MICHAEL SABATINO,
PATRICK MULDOON,
CHRISTIE CLARK &
ALISON SWEENEY

$1.19   Canada $1.29

This is my first *Soap* magazine cover shoot ever. I have to laugh, thinking back on how my parents were horrified by how revealing my dress was!

Shooting "Alan the rapist" was my first big story on *Days*. What an entrance.

The magazine cover shown:

WALT SHARES HIS HIDDEN TALENT!

WIN $500

SOAP OPERA UPDATE

DAYS EXPLODES!
All The HOTTEST Stories!
Sami's Plot Backfires!

ALL MY CHILDREN
Michael Knight Reveals The Secrets Of Daytime

Why Soap Schemers Get A Second Chance

THE YOUNG & THE RESTLESS
Intrigue And Romance On Location

David, Joey & Dylan / OLTL
LLANVIEW MEN TELL ALL

JAN. 24, 1995 $2.50 CANADA $2.95

Austin, Carrie, Sami & Kim / DAYS

ON-AIR SWEAR WORD ENRAGES FANS

SOAP OPERA DIGEST

NOVEMBER 9, 1999

EVERY SHOW EVERY WEEK

It's Contract Time: Which Stars Will *Walk*

DAYS OF OUR LIVES

COVERS TO CHOOSE FROM

Austin Chooses Sami!

BEHIND THE SCENES

WITH SOAPS' HOTTEST TEENS!

$2.99

4 5 >

0 86441 18207 9

Austin Peck took over the role of "Austin" in 1995. Christie and I both thought he was such a hunk!

FAMILY TREES FOR ALL THE SHOWS!

FEBRUARY 13, 1996

SOAP OPERA DIGEST

SHOCKING DAYS AHEAD

- •Watch Out For Billie!
- •John & Marlena...
- •Sami Gets Her Man

WEDDING PREVIEW
WHO WILL SAY "I DO"

$2.69

07

0 14014 18207 2

Here's the classic Sami cover line—Sami spent nine years chasing after Austin!

Bryan, Christie and I worked together for almost nine years. Austin was there for almost seven. It's amazing how time flies, huh?

Why ❸ Stars Really Left

JUNE 4, 1996

SOAP
OPER
DIGE!

VCR
ALERT:
Can't-Miss
Episodes!

DAYS OF OUR LIVES
Watch Out,
Sami...
You're
About
To Get
Caught!

Soaps'
Worst
Boyfriends

$2.69

23 >

0 14014 18207 2

I never spent a lot of time smiling at photo
shoots—Sami was either smirking or unhappy!

#1 NEWS WEEKLY

SUSAN BATTEN REPLACES ATWT'S ALLYSON RICE-TAYLOR
EDDIE CIBRIAN TAKES OVER FOR ASHLEY HAMILTON ON SUNSET

SOAP OPERA WEEKLY

VOLUME 6 ISSUE 9   MARCH 4, 1997

NEWS FLASH

WILL GH'S SONNY AND BRENDA SURVIVE SHOOT-OUT?

SPECIAL 27-PAGE SECTION

SOAP OPERA'S **50 most beautiful people**

THE **PUPPET MASTER**
When Sami pulls the strings, Salem dances!
PLUS The actors reveal what they'd like to see happen

$2.49   Canada $2.95

Yup—Sami pulling the
strings. Can you believe
that "lion's mane" of
hair? All I can say is it
was the '90s!

A huge part of Sami's character are her insecurities. I've always been able to hide mine in my character.

DAYTIME ACTRESS DUBBED DEADBEAT MOM!

SoapOperaWeekly

FREE POSTER AND CALENDAR INSIDE

SEPTEMBER 9, 2003

JEANNE COOPER

SON LANDS MAJOR ROLE ON Y&R!

• OLTL FAVE RETURNS
• STUNNING CANCELLATION TWIST

SHOCKERS!

Y&R: THE UNTHINKABLE HAPPENS

DAYS: A NEW SAMI!

$2.99
Canada $3.99

www.soapoperaweekly.com

ALL NBC

SOAPS

IN DEPTH

MISSY REEVES The Latest On Her Return To NBC!

DAYS

WILL NEVER BE THE SAME AGAIN!

Will Sami Win Austin From Carrie... Or Lose Her Freedom?

AW: Cass Vows To Protect Lila!

SUN: Can Cole Save Caitlin In Time?

$2.99 • CANADA $3.75
NOVEMBER 17, 1998

As Sami continued to wreak havoc in Salem, I grew up and started showing a more mature side of myself and my character.

Sami's big breakthrough. Her time on death row really turned Sami into a woman. Sami's execution was one of the most challenging stories I've had to play on *Days*.

You'll notice in this photo I have very little make-up on. I really wanted Sami to seem as young and "innocent" as possible. Though soaps are famous for actresses always looking glamorous, I wanted to have as little make-up as I could through all these scenes. The make-up department was thrilled that I wanted to stay "real"!

I laughed when I first saw the cover line. "Size Matters" could be misinterpreted, but once reading the article, fans saw that I was very openly discussing my weight loss and how difficult it is to struggle with diet.

Woman's World was the perfect opportunity to spread my message to more fans. I feel so strongly about promoting a healthy mental image for women, and I was glad to have this opportunity.

SPECIAL EDITION

$1.99

soap digest

OPERA

THE TRUE INSIDER GUIDE

MAY 21, 2002

THE Diet ISSUE

- Before And After Photos
- Secrets To Dressing "Thin"
- How Actresses Drop Pregnancy Pounds
- Plus-Size Star: Live A Little!

Talk Of Return For GH's Vanessa Marcil!

PLUS: EMMY SPECIAL!

DAYS's Alison Sweeney Cried When Fans Called Her Fat. LOOK AT HER NOW!

Display Until 5/21/02
$1.99 Canada $1.99

21>

0 75470 08185 9

Soap Opera Digest has always been a big supporter, and I was thrilled to be offered the chance to talk about my weight loss and what the fan reaction had been like.

Austin always used to tickle me when we were doing really serious poses at photo shoots. It's funny to me how "serious" we all look here since I know we were laughing between each shot.

Matt Cedeno and I had such fun working together. He is such a great guy, a talented actor and let's face it—a total hottie!

L.A. Brides

$1.95
Spring/Summer 2000

Great Places to Say "I Do"

Hassle-Free Wedding Planning

Unforgettable Wedding Cakes

Honeymoon in Mendocino

Alison Sweeney

I posed for *L.A. Brides* during my engagement to Dave. It was so much fun trying on all different types of wedding gowns to help me figure out which one I wanted in real life.

This is the first "Lumi" cover! Bryan and I did a really fun set-up at the shoot where we got to spray water hoses at each other. We had so much fun soaking each other!

Judi and I got to hang out and chat during this photo shoot. Since it was a "Diet" issue, I'm sure you can imagine what the topics were . . . dieting, eating, exercising, etc. We swapped our weight-issue stories.

bond, and I braced myself to play Sami as she had never been seen before.

The scriptwriters sure didn't disappoint. Sami started by getting a hotel room next to Carrie and Austin's honeymoon suite, and in behavior that might have qualified her for a job with the CIA, she spied on them having sex. At one point, she even concealed herself under their bed (could it get any kinkier?!).

Shall I continue? There were several false starts that could have brought Sami and Austin back together, perhaps for good. (Wait—is anything "for good" in Salem?) However, there were always unexpected, last-minute speed bumps that arose in Sami's path that disrupted any fantasies that she had for a lifelong relationship with Austin. As recently as 2002, Sami was once again on the brink of marrying Austin, this time in Las Vegas. She had finally won the man of her dreams, the man she had been chasing for years—or at least that's what she thought. But just before the couple was about to recite their wedding vows, Austin overheard Sami talking to Lucas, and describing all of her deceit and lies to win Austin's heart. My line (or actually Sami's) was, "Austin's never going to find out the truth. He believed me then and he'll believe me now!"

Well, Sami, not exactly. Austin was stunned by Sami's unwitting confession, and their wedding plans dissolved instantly. The next step was an easy one for Austin: He stood her up at the altar, furious over her dishonesty and ignoring her desperate pleas for forgiveness. There were two episodes where a heartbroken Sami fruitlessly begged Austin to take her back, pleading, "I don't regret what I did because I did it for love. I did it because I love you."

That girl is really something, isn't she? Austin turned a

deaf ear, rode out of town, and left Sami to bake alone in the Las Vegas sun. The best part of it for those viewers who find watching Sami as appealing as the sound of fingernails on a chalkboard is that she always does it to herself. It's such beautiful justice that her own words did her in, silencing her smugness, at least for a while.

Sibling Rivalry to the Max

As you've already surmised, Carrie and Sami were like oil and water. It's hard to think of two sisters who had more contempt for one another (and so different than the relationship I had with my two real-life brothers). Christie Clark (who played Carrie) and I are actually friends in real life—when I first started on the show, she was like an older sister who took care of me—but you'd never know it by our bitter on-screen relationship and an occasional slap, smack, or slug here and there.

Of course, Sami has been involved in many other feuds along the way, including her long-time battle with Kate (played by Lauren Koslow), who more than once tried to expose Sami for her many schemes—although most of the time, Sami was able to tap-dance her way out of it, somehow turning the tables to make Kate look bad for saying the things she did. *(My personal take is that Kate and Sami have always been similar types of people. So that means that they'll either be best friends or they'll hate each other. In this case, Salem wasn't big enough for both of them, and their nonstop feud was almost inevitable.)*

But back to that memorable *Days* scene when Sami's scheming for Austin became more than Carrie could stand,

and she unloaded on Sami with a slap heard 'round the
world—or at least 'round TV sets in every part of the
world! The truth can be told that Christie and I rehearsed
that slap sequence a number of times, and she was never
supposed to make contact with my cheek. During the rehearsal, we moved at what is called "half speed," showing
the cameramen what was going to happen so they'd be
able to follow the action. In true Hollywood fashion,
Christie was supposed to swing, miss my face by at least
two or three inches, and I was supposed to stumble back-
ward like Muhammad Ali had just landed a right jab on
my chin (fortunately, thanks to camera angles and good
acting, you don't have to actually strike someone to make
it look like the real thing). Well, everything went fine in rehearsals—but with the camera rolling and the bright lights
turned on, it was a different story. We had never practiced
the scene standing on our marks (I realized afterwards),
and when it really counted, Christie was closer to me than
she had been during our practice sessions. So when she
swung, my face got in the way of her hand's trajectory.

Christie's hand planted a hard slap right onto my cheek.
I certainly wasn't expecting to be hit, and it literally spun
me around. I lost my balance and tumbled over. On the
way to the floor, my head banged into a nearby piano. I
may have used a four-letter word or two on my way down.
(If I did, I plead "temporary insanity"!)

Now, in the script, I was supposed to be knocked out
cold by Carrie's slap. Well, for a few moments there, I
wondered whether method acting had come to *Days*, and
whether I was really about to lose consciousness!

Of course, it wasn't intentional (Right, Christie?). While
I'm at it, I must tell you that Bryan (my dear, sweet, sup-

portive friend) thought it was hysterical that I was cursing like a sailor. He literally ran off the set holding his hand over his mouth so that I wouldn't hear him laughing at me! I have managed to forgive him for his treacherous behavior, and now I definitely have a sense of humor about the whole thing. But the camera guys still tease me about it.

Before the piano stopped resonating, production called a "five." Once I regrouped, we reshot the scene, and this time it went according to plan (for which I'm eternally grateful!). Take Two was the one that audiences saw when the show aired. In the meantime, if you ever need a sparring partner, Christie might be a perfect choice!

Driving Sami up the Wall

I know that over the years, Sami has deserved her share of slaps (as well as a clenched fist or two on occasion). But perhaps nothing can compare to the pounding she took from Austin—or to be more accurate, from Austin's car. Now, playing Sami, I'm used to portraying a character who lives life on the edge. I've been called on to do a lot of crazy things in Sami-land, but when they told me that I'd be hit by a car driven by Austin—or, more accurately, hit by his car *twice!*—it did get my attention.

Poor Sami really was hit by Austin's car and slammed into a wall. It happened on New Year's Eve, not long after Sami had decided to take Austin's car and he had reported it stolen. She finally returned it to the police station, where Austin retrieved it. But as he drove away, the car accidentally shifted into reverse and struck Sami, propelling her into the wall—more than once! (I can only imagine what

Sami's New Year's resolution was at that moment—perhaps just to live to see January 2nd!)

Now, by this point, fans were very familiar with (and perhaps sick of) Sami and her insane shenanigans, and probably some of them would have loved to have seen Austin's car screeching at about 90 miles per hour or more right at me. In fact, you won't believe some of the letters I received after that episode. One of my "fans" wrote, "Too bad he didn't hit you a third time!" (Ah, the warm feelings that Sami stirs in our viewers!)

Sami did survive her run-in with Austin's car, but just barely. She underwent emergency surgery at Salem University Hospital, had a near-death experience that would give anyone the shivers, and finally awoke from her coma, thanks in part to a guilt-ridden Austin sitting for hours by her bedside. When she awoke, she was suffering from amnesia and temporary paralysis below the waist.

Let me tell you, lying in that hospital bed playing a critically injured Sami was a real challenge. Every day, I was fitted with bandages around my head, a collar around my neck, needles in my arm, IV drips overhead and an oxygen tube helping me breathe. For weeks, my most stylish attire was a hospital gown!

It wasn't exactly how you picture glamorous soaps!

During this time, as Sami struggled with amnesia, she convinced Austin to marry her for the sake of Will, who she believed to be their son (at least at the moment). But when her memory returned, and she realized that Austin hadn't fathered her baby after all, she decided to fake that she still had amnesia—and we were on our way toward another of *Days'* famous wedding days.

Plans for that Sami-Austin wedding actually moved forward, right up to the day of the ceremony. But just moments before their marriage was to become official and with Sami dressed in an absolutely gorgeous wedding gown, Carrie burst into the chapel to halt the proceedings and deliver a literal knockout punch to Sami's wedding plans—and to her cheek![3] Carrie and Eric (Sami's twin) had unearthed the information that Lucas, not Austin, was really Will's father. As you can guess, after Carrie's slap the wedding plans instantly dissolved.

As I've written, Lucas was furious about being deceived. When he learned that he, not Austin, was the father, he made a decision that would create absolute chaos in Sami's life: He fought for the custody of little Will. I'm sure the lawyers on both sides—and their bank accounts—couldn't have been happier with all the legal maneuvering!

Up on the Roof

If you need any more examples of Sami's manipulating mind, let me take you back in time to one of my favorite Sami schemes, designed to drive Carrie and Austin apart. It unfolded when the couple was already having trouble in their relationship, largely because of Sami's conniving (there's a surprise!). At one point, Carrie and Austin arranged to meet on their apartment building roof at exactly midnight on New Year's Eve. They decided that if one of them didn't show up, they'd know that their relationship was over.

Well, in a bit of skillful eavesdropping, Sami overheard them making their plan, and she immediately devised a

---

3. No actresses were injured in the shooting of this scene.

sinister plot: She snuck into Austin's apartment, and changed his clocks so he would show up on the roof an hour after midnight—long after Carrie had come and gone. And that's exactly what happened. Carrie arrived on the roof at midnight, found herself alone, and returned to her room brokenhearted over the apparent end of her relationship with Austin. Sami came by to "console" her sister, although in no time, Lucas burst into the apartment, obviously drunk. Within minutes, he passed out and the girls put him in Carrie's bed.

That's when Sami's wild conniving took over. She slipped a sleeping pill into her sister's glass of New Year's champagne, and when Carrie collapsed, she dragged her into bed next to Lucas. Before long, Austin arrived at Carrie's apartment, and Sami made sure that he saw Lucas and Carrie in bed together. Austin was stunned. In his mind, not only did Carrie not show up on the roof at midnight, but she had decided to sleep with Lucas instead! That caused plenty of agony between Carrie and Austin until they figured out what Sami had done.

It is so much fun doing scenes like that—putting drugs in people's drinks and dragging Christie Clark across the floor to the bed. These just aren't things that happen in real life (thank goodness!).

Other Men, Other Mayhem

Even though Austin was the man who Sami obsessed over for years, there have been other men in her life, which has given me the chance to do plenty of romantic scenes with other cast members of *Days*. How about Brandon Walker

(played by Matt Cedeno) for example? In one story line
back in 2000, Brandon and Sami schemed to infiltrate the
mob that hung out at a local strip club, all as part of a
greater (and elaborate) plan that would ruin Lucas's credi-
bility and give Sami sole custody of Will. Brandon came up
with the idea that he'd play a pimp, and Sami would dress
up as a hooker in order to penetrate the circle of gangsters.
To her credit, Sami wasn't too keen on the idea, but after
finally agreeing to go along with it, she tried out some pretty
outrageous outfits in Brandon's apartment—with him as
an audience of one—to get just the right woman-of-the-
night look (after all, what does the well-dressed Salem
streetwalker wear these days?). Before long, Brandon and
Sami were dancing together, and the heat in the apartment
got well past the boiling point. Before long, he planted a
passionate kiss on Sami's lips (wow!), and she was completely swept away. There was an intense attraction between these two. For weeks, fans wondered whether Sami
would abandon her feelings for Austin and give in to her
desires for Brandon.

But I don't have to tell you that relationships are never
simple in Salem (thank goodness, or people might stop
watching!). Sami and Brandon continued to draw closer
together, and as their attraction became more passionate,
Lucas and Kate developed a scheme of their own against
Sami, with Kate determined to drive Sami haywire. While
they were all in Italy, Kate convinced Lucas to lace Sami's
salad with a mind-altering herb while Sami was having
dinner with Brandon at Moroni's restaurant. Lucas succeeded in tainting the salad, but there was much more of
the hallucinogen than anyone realized. Before long, Sami
had slipped into a frightening drug-induced state. She began

convulsing. She was having difficulty breathing. She had some terrifying hallucinations and flashbacks, not to mention a seizure or two.

Well, as you've guessed by now, Sami pulled through. The incident was just one more time when she extricated herself from the jaws of death. But who would want it any other way? After all, without Sami around, there would be one fewer person to create chaos in Salem, and no one wants that, right?

The good news is that the perils of Sami keep *Days'* fans glued to their TV screens to find out what's going to happen next. If you've been one of those loyal viewers, year after year, the high ratings sure have made the producers and network happy! So thanks!

(Author's personal collection)

My brothers are so important to me. Through all our childhood pranks and endless teasing, we've always been there for each other. Every year my dad gathers us up, and we take family photos for Christmas cards and stuff. Here are two of those photos.

Chapter 9

As I've written, *Days of Our Lives* often deals with topical issues in very realistic ways. That was certainly the case when the story line concentrated on the subject of rape, which is one of the worst of all possible nightmares for girls and women. Just the thought of it is terrifying. But early in my career on *Days of Our Lives*, when I was barely 16 years old, I had to live through a rape through my character, Sami. It is as close as I ever want to come to the real thing.

In the scene, I was assaulted by the character Alan (played by Paul Kersey, a really nice guy in real life!). He had originally targeted Carrie, but Austin (who was then Carrie's boyfriend) intervened before Alan could do any damage. So he turned his attention to Sami, whom he had actually dated as a way to get closer to Carrie. (I know I told you part of this story in the previous chapter, so bear with me as I give you more details.)

The plot thickens. Sami was cooking dinner for Alan at

his apartment. But the evening unraveled for Sami very quickly. Before long, Alan had duped her into posing for some suggestive photographs. Then before she knew what was happening, he suddenly and unexpectedly became physical with her. She clearly said "no," but he held her down on his sofa and raped her. The story line was that Alan was so outraged over being rejected by Carrie that he turned his fury on Sami, and he showed no mercy. Yes, it was only acting, but for me it was a very scary experience.

As you can imagine, the rape scene was very physical and very violent, and I really had no frame of reference on what to expect. As the cameras rolled, Paul held me down on the sofa, gripping my wrists with one of his hands and holding my arms over my head. The director had instructed me to fight back while Paul was sitting on my stomach, kissing me, and ripping my blouse with his free hand. Believe me, I fought that guy with everything I had. I could feel Sami's terror with every fiber of my being. I resisted. I kicked. I bucked. I screamed. I tried to get free of his grip in any way I could, using literally every ounce of strength that I had. But I couldn't get him off. I couldn't budge him at all.

The sad truth is that if Paul had wanted to, he could have held me there all day, and there was nothing I could have done. I was completely at his mercy. Yes, all along I knew that we were acting, but as I became swept up in the panic that Sami was feeling, it was shocking to realize just how helpless I was. In an actual rape, the terror must be multiplied a million times!

When the director finally yelled "Cut," Paul climbed off of me and I was so relieved to be free of his control. There was a short break in the shooting at that point, and everyone must have sensed just how difficult it had been for me. One of the cameramen tried to lighten the mood by saying "We'll get him for you, Ali! Just let me at 'em!" It made me feel instantly better to be reminded that it was only a scene, and that I was surrounded by friends. But I still sat there stunned for quite a while. During the five-minute break, I remained by myself on the set, just trying to collect my thoughts. I had so closely identified with what Sami was going through that I felt completely traumatized by the experience. I felt violated. I felt assaulted. It was so scary, especially since I was sixteen years old. Those feelings of terror lingered, long after the scene had been shot.

Here's something else that I found quite remarkable: That experience really affected how I thought of men for a while. I became very careful (and I still am) about being alone with men whom I don't completely trust. The whole thing was pretty creepy!

In that *Days* story line, Sami didn't tell anyone what had happened in the immediate aftermath of the rape. But Lucas eventually discovered the provocative photos of Sami in Alan's wallet, and she finally divulged that he had raped her. What an upheaval in Salem! Before long, Carrie had convinced Sami to bring charges against Alan, and a very traumatized Sami testified against him. But there just wasn't enough evidence to convict him. To make matters worse for Sami, a tabloid published the alluring photos of her! She was publicly humiliated, and in her despair, she tried to retreat from the public eye.

What happened next? Well, Alan remained furious at Sami. He pursued her with more sinister motives in mind. At one point, face to face, he threatened her with a gun and there was a violent scuffle. Sami somehow gained control of the weapon—and in the chaos of the moment, she shot him. The bullet struck Alan in a rather sensitive area—well, let's just say that after the shooting, it would have been very difficult for Alan to enjoy an active sex life. The Salem tabloid that had attacked Sami during the trial came up with a memorable headline after the shooting: "Sami Brady Bobbittizes Alan Harris."

Ah, sweet revenge!

All You Need Is Love

As difficult as the rape scene was for me, I'm fortunate in that I've had many more on-screen scenes that have been completely romantic! (Nice transition, huh?!) I've been in plenty of love scenes on *Days*, but they do take some getting used to. Some have definitely been embarrassing, particularly when I was younger. But you do what you have to do (or as the cliché goes, "It's a tough job, but somebody's gotta do it!"). Love scenes are always easier when they're with an actor who makes it easy for you. But no matter what the circumstances, it's part of the job, and you do eventually get the hang of it. I'm an actress, and whether the script calls for a love scene or one that involves a rape, you do what the writers and director ask for.

For the love scenes—well, imagine what those rehearsals are like! Actually, I've always made an effort to keep the rehearsals as relaxed and lighthearted as possible, having a little fun with the other actors and crew members and making sure no one is feeling tense or uptight (particularly me!). It's such a balancing act: You try to stay relaxed, and stay emotionally in character, but at the same time there are so many things to be aware of. Once the cameras are rolling, there's definitely no playing around. Love scenes are similar to dance scenes—both are carefully choreographed! And the cast and crew are all involved. Since the woman is often wearing something skimpy, both the cameramen and the actress have to be aware of not showing *too* much! The actors have to follow very specific direction about where to kiss and what angle to position their bodies, and the cameras have to be in the right spot at the right moment to get the perfect angle on each movement. There's a job to do, and it couldn't get done without the complete professionalism of the crewmembers and the cast. (Now in revealing all this inside information, I hope I haven't ruined for you the romance of the next love scene you watch. We want you to forget about all the hard work that went into it, and enjoy the story!!!)

As you might guess, the same is true with highly dramatic, highly emotional scenes. During rehearsals, the cast and the crew remain pretty serious, giving the actors room to reach the emotional peak called for in the scene. It can get pretty tense. At times, you really can hear a pin drop!

Then, once the actual taping begins, the mood is absolutely dead serious. Sure, there are occasional funny moments where an actor flubs a line or a slap actually hits the intended target when it was supposed to miss by a few inches (I'll never let Christie forget that one! . . . Just kidding!). As you might imagine, we sometimes crack one another up because of something that happens unexpectedly. But in general, everyone's pretty thoughtful, making sure the scene turns out perfectly.

Here's one lighter incident that comes to mind: Miriam

Parrish was playing Jamie Caldwell, and we had a scene together where we were outside a women's rest room and overheard a bulimic woman vomiting behind the door. Our task was to *pretend* that we were actually hearing and reacting to the unsettling sounds of a woman throwing up, although the actual noises associated with the vomiting were going to be dubbed in later. But suddenly, coming over the loudspeaker, there was a very loud, graphic, and realistic soundtrack of someone vomiting, followed by a toilet flushing. Miriam and I looked at one another. The sound effects had caught both of us by surprise. It was only seconds until we could no longer keep a straight face. We really tried! But sure enough, our composure didn't last, and we laughed uncontrollably. We had absolutely lost it!

Take two!

Some actors on *Days* are more prone than others to break up laughing when something strikes them funny, but in general, we try to keep the interruptions and distractions to a minimum. With our tight schedule, we just don't have the time. Not long after I joined the show, there was a little "Brady family dance" that we'd do whenever we completed a scene in just one take. I think Deidre and Wayne came up with it, and it caught on. One time, it even appeared on the show in an ice skating scene, with all of us dancing around the pond as if the Bradys had taken leave of our senses. It became our way of saying, "Yes! We did it the first time!"

Of course, everyone blows a line from time to time, and while it might be amusing enough to make it onto Dick Clark's "bloopers" show now and then, stumbling over your dialogue time after time is not the way to win friends and influence people (particularly if those people are your fellow actors or directors!). With the time crunch we're usually under, those retakes can test everyone's patience. After you mess up four or five times, you might be laughing nervously, but the people around you may be ready to punch you out! The crew is probably dying to take a break, and you're working on take six! Get the picture?

All in the Family

Whether we're taping difficult scenes like the rape episode, or doing scenes that are much more routine, one of the great things about working on *Days of Our Lives* is having the support of so many wonderful fellow actors. You hear so much about jealousies and back-stabbing in Hollywood, and I'm sure some of that goes on. It must be such a drag. Fortunately, I've never seen it on the set of *Days*. In fact, some of my closest friends are the actors who, like me, call *Days* their home.

I've always felt that our cast and crew are part of a big family (sure, it sounds corny, but it's really true!). You can't help but feel close to people you work with for so many long hours and share such enjoyable—and at times stressful and challenging—experiences. During scenes that are particularly demanding, it's amazing how supportive everyone is, helping you work through it and reach your potential as an actor. All of us want *Days* to continue as the excellent show that it is, and so we want *everyone* on the soap to succeed. It's not unusual to complete a difficult scene, and have fellow actors come up to you and say, "I saw that scene you did; you were *so* good in it!" Imagine how great that makes you feel! Yes, all of us (by necessity) are preoccupied with our own story lines, and we don't have a lot of time just to "hang out" with cast members that we don't work with a lot. But when we do get a chance to watch each other, we're the first to give each other a high five! It really is a wonderful environment to work in!

I think this closeness is very important, and we're so lucky to have such tight relationships that have allowed the show to grow with so little envy and resentment. We've all heard rumors about actors on other shows who sometimes think or say, "Why does she get more camera time than I do?" But *Days* is different. It's a true ensemble show where everyone gets his or her time to shine. And we work too hard, and have too strong a commitment to *Days*, to let pettiness get in the way of producing the best possible show.

Who are my closest friends on *Days*? They're really the

(Author's personal collection)

A bunch of us girls at the *Days of Our Lives* anniversary party

actors who I work with repeatedly on one story line after another. Take Arianne Zuker, for example. On the show, Ari plays Nicole, who is Sami's bitter rival. It seems that Nicole and Sami are always screaming at one another and raking each other over the coals. It's simply their modus operandi. But off camera, it's really a different story. Ari is absolutely great and one of my closest friends! The on-camera battles and bitchiness are purely acting. In fact, Ari and I have plenty of fun playing enemies on the show, really getting a kick out of the bad blood between our characters, and finding ways to make our on-screen relationship as wicked as possible! But I wish you could see us rehearsing in one another's dressing rooms. We often crack each other up, finding ourselves in stitches over the venomous dialogue coming from our lips; once we're on the set, however, we put on our game faces, and get through the scenes with as much animosity and hatred as we can muster.

Ari is just one of my close friends on the show, and I don't have the space to write about each of them. But let me tell you, because *Days* is a soap, cast members often leave the show and then return—and it's so great when a true friend comes back. Bryan Dattilo played Lucas for many years—he and I started on the show at about the same time, but his character disappeared from *Days* (it happens all the time on soaps!) for a short time, only to return in 2002. Over the years, Bryan and I have had so many fun scenes together, whether we're being affectionate or we're at each other's throats. He and I have had our share of very physical scenes—we're either fighting (Sami has choked Lucas on several occasions), or I'm passed out and he's saving my life (My hero!). We've been together on camera so many times over the years that sometimes a word or a line will remind us of something funny that's happened in the past, and we'll both break up laughing. It's been so much fun to work with him again.

By the way, Bryan is not only a close friend, but also one of the funniest people I've ever known. At various times, he's played pranks on me—from placing Vaseline on my dressing room doorknob, to putting gel in my telephone. (It's OK, Bryan, I forgive you! . . . Boys will be boys!) And of course, I got him back!

Before I forget, I have to mention that one of the most enjoyable experiences I've had on the show is working with the boys who have played Sami's son, Will. As you may know, when Sami gave birth to her baby, the infant was played by twin boys, Shawn and Taylor Carpenter, starting when they were just six weeks old. Over the years, I had a wonderful relationship with them, both in front of and behind the cameras. They are such sweet and special children, and it was so great watching them grow up. They were always a blast to work with, and quite amazingly, even at a very young age they seemed to know when to be quiet and when to let loose. They somehow knew when the cameras were rolling and when they needed to be silent. As they became older and they had lines to speak, it was sometimes hard to get them to talk because they were so used to being still and quiet. But everything changed as soon as they walked off the set; they became totally normal kids—running, shouting, playing games with us, and jumping all over Austin Peck as if he were a jungle gym. Like I said, boys will be boys!

In particular, I remember a scene I had with Shawn when the twins were just infants. The script called for me to become really emotional, crying hysterically, and speaking a long, tear-stained monologue while standing over him in his crib. Well, Shawn looked up and saw me crying, just as the script called for. But my tears really upset him, and *he* started crying and screaming, too. The two of us were quite a sight, each of us sobbing and bawling, as if trying to upstage one another!

Shawn, of course, had been used to seeing me laughing and joking, and certainly didn't understand that I was only acting or pretending. Through my tears, I could see how frightened he was, and as the cameras continued to run, I instinctively reached down, picked him up and tried to comfort him. All the while, I continued speaking my lines, but tried to make them sound a little less painful so the baby would calm down. It actually made for a very powerful scene. As Sami, I was putting my child's needs first, dealing sensitively with his emotions, no matter what I was going through.

I recall one particularly memorable episode not long after Lucas discovered that he was Will's real dad. In this scene, Lucas leaped to the head of the class when it came to clumsiness. In the script, he *dropped* Will while rough-housing with him—specifically, while playing "airplane" with his son. (Don't worry, no babies were harmed in the filming of this episode!) On the show, Sami became furious, convinced that the lump on Will's head occurred when Lucas struck the boy in a drunken stupor. Sami, ever the protective mom, was so angry that she was determined to press charges.

No matter how evil or sinister Sami's behavior has been at times, she has always absolutely adored her son. When it comes to being a mom, she's the real deal! Even Sami has redeeming qualities!

Eventually, Shawn and Taylor fell victim to the "rapid aging syndrome," where *Days'* producers decided to replace the boys (at about age six) with a ten-year-old (the role of Will is now played by the adorable Christopher Gerse). It happens a lot in soap operas, where characters become several years older literally overnight. Once you agree to watch a soap opera, you agree to suspend rational thinking from time to time. (It happened to Sami, by the way, when the actress who played her before me—Christina Wagoner—left the show in 1992 at the age of nine, and I took over the role the following year when I was sixteen years old!). While they were on the show, Shawn and Taylor were wonderful to work with, and it was sad to see them leave.

A Little "Sibling" Support

Let me close this chapter talking about two other very important characters on *Days of Our Lives*. As you know, while I have two wonderful brothers in real life, I'm the only daughter in the family. But I've had two "sisters" on *Days*—Carrie and Belle—and I have felt very close to both of them. Of course, when you're talking about Christie Clark (who played Carrie for many years), our characters were at each other's throats for most of our time on the show together. But off camera, Christie definitely fulfilled the role of a surrogate sister. We spent a lot of time teasing and joking with one another about the amazing messes our characters got themselves into. In real life, however, I turned to Christie for advice on many occasions. I felt like I could tell her anything, and she definitely shared some of her own life experiences with me as well. (Thanks, Christie!)

And then there's Kirsten Storms, who plays my little sister, Belle. We have a great and supportive relationship, and like any sibling, she asks for my advice from time to time about matters both on and off the small screen. I remember the time she had planned to cook dinner for her real-life boyfriend, and she asked for my help. Together, we came up with a menu—Kirsten told me what they liked to eat, we developed the recipes and all the ingredients, and I gave her advice on everything from chopping vegetables to sautéing. It was so cool to have her ask me, and it was so much fun to help.

That's what friends (and "sisters") are for.

We're so lucky to enjoy this kind of camaraderie on the show, and it has always been that way. Just ask Frances Reid, who has been a mainstay on the show from the beginning. She was in the very first episode of *Days* (although as she points out, another actress played Alice Horton in the pilot for the show). Frances is such a wonderful woman and a talented actress, and I've been so fortunate to have worked with her for so many years.

From the beginning, when I was just a teenager, several of the show's actors took me under their wing and became like older brothers to me. They looked out for me, always asking if I had any questions or concerns, and wanted to make sure I was enjoying the experience of being part of the large ensemble cast. Actors like Drake Hogestyn and Josh Taylor (ex-Roman) in particular played a very fatherly role. Drake, for example, who plays John Black, has always been so thoughtful and sincere in his interest in my experiences on *Days* and in my life in general. Drake is such a great dad in real life—he talks about his daughters and son all the time—and his caring and compassion sure come through in his work on the show. When Drake and I have scenes together, he has this wonderful paternal way about him, and while Sami is often being ruthless and bitchy, I end up thinking, "What a great dad! I can't believe I'm so mean to him!"

Even I cringe once in a while at some of the meaner and more evil things that Sami says, especially to John and Marlena. Of course, at the same time that I'm thinking, "I can't say that—it's so mean!", Melissa Reeves or Deidre Hall may tell me, "What do you mean, you don't want to say that line—I wish I had lines like that." They may relish the opportunity to be mean once in a while, whereas I'm mean all the time! Ah, the life of Sami!

Chapter 10

These are lean times in Hollywood.

No, I'm not referring to the scarcity of jobs that actors are up against, which relegate too many of my peers into unemployment lines or into gotta-pay-the-bills jobs as waitresses or temp secretaries. Instead, I'm thinking of a different kind of "lean times"—namely, the super-skinny actresses who are more razor-thin than ever these days, and are dying to be even leaner (in some cases, almost *literally* dying!). You know who I'm talking about—those actresses who nearly seem to disappear when they turn sideways, and whose daily caloric intake seems to be their answer to the question, "How low can you go?" Some of them look so fragile that an unexpected gust of wind just might take them for the ride of their lives!

Okay, maybe I'm exaggerating a little—but not by much. So many actresses are convinced that their career success depends on much more than their acting talents. The party line is that they better stay as skinny as possible for as long as possible because there are hundreds, perhaps thousands, of reed-thin actresses eager to take their place. As a result, the obsession with thinness has become rampant throughout every part of the entertainment industry. True story.

Striving to be Hollywood-thin has been practically an obsession with me since I hit puberty. And as an actress who loves my job on *Days of Our Lives* and hopes to continue acting for many more years, I can't ignore what casting agents are looking for—and it seems that for most roles, they're hungering for the slimmest, most svelte actresses they can find. People say that the television camera makes you look ten pounds heavier, so the actresses who appear almost gaunt and skeletal often win the attention of Hollywood decision-makers at the expense of those who have a more wholesome, healthy look. If you see an actress who appears thin on TV, imagine what she looks like face-to-face!

As tragic as it sounds, the industry standards support the passion of some actresses to become anorexic or bulimic because the camera's eye will make them look "normal," not underweight. So they torture their bodies and souls, all so they can do what they love, which is acting.

In this chapter and the three that follow, I'll give you my point of view on show business's preoccupation with weight, and how I've finally dealt with it in a positive way in my own life.

Thin Is In

What effect does Hollywood's weight obsession have on actresses like me? It's so easy to get caught up in the "thin-is-in" ethos, which is why so many of my colleagues are totally preoccupied with the number on the scale and do whatever they have to do to keep it from moving in an upward direction. They eat like birds (anorexic birds at that!). They routinely skip meals. Some of them take laxatives. They've turned near-starvation into an art form.

Before I go any further, I will say that there are a number of women I know who are thin naturally. My friend and costar, Ari (Nicole), is a perfect example of a beautiful, super-model-type figure, and she doesn't have to work at it at all. I know what you're thinking—I hate her, too! ☺ But seriously, even though she has genetics on her side, she makes an effort to be healthy, to work out, and to take care of herself. In fact, she has to work to keep weight *on*! My point is, there is a body type that is naturally thin— and I'm not talking about those women. I'm talking instead about the women who fight their figures throughout their whole careers, and in some cases take that fight to extremes.

Growing up in the entertainment industry, I've known actresses who vomit after almost every meal. For some of the thinnest-of-the-thin actresses, it's as much a part of their routine as brushing their teeth and putting on make-up—they seem to feel that they can't afford to backslide, can't afford to gain even a single pound or two. Physical appearance is everything. More than once, I've walked into a rest room at a Hollywood studio or at a restaurant with a show business clientele and heard an actress in the bathroom stall, throwing up her lunch. Yuck! Almost everyone in the industry pretends that nothing is wrong. But they've got to be kidding. I've known actresses who seem like they're about to collapse because they're so malnourished (I really mean that!). If she's a teenage actress, someone in the production company may whisper something to her mom—but even parents are often in denial. Too often, moms in particular are part of the problem, encouraging their actress-daughters to count calories and watch their weight until it becomes pathological. It is so frightening!

Can you think of any other business or industry in the world that leads girls and women into this kind of self-destructive behavior? Well, okay, I mean besides ballet and gymnastics?

How disturbing do the stories get? Just picture this. Not long ago, a photographer told me about a day-long fashion shoot he had just done with a well-known supermodel who had set new standards for thinness (just take a look at the models in any issue of *Vogue* or *Harper's Bazaar*, and you'll know what I mean). During the shoot, there was plenty of food available for the photographer, his assistants, the makeup artists, the agent, the manager—and the model. But while everyone else was eating generous portions and going back for seconds, the model didn't touch *any* of the catered food. Probably obsessed with maintaining her figure, she had brought her own lunch—a sunflower seed! That's right. *One* sunflower seed. While others on the set couldn't resist the generous spread of food during breaks and during the lunch hour, she could have carried her meal for the day in a thimble!

Later, the photographer told me, "It's hard to believe, but the only thing she ate during the entire six hours was the sunflower seed! That's it. During the course of the day, she fainted three times under the bright lights. She was starving herself. It was unbelievable."

Is that scary or what?!

There are a lot of stories just like that. A few of them may be urban legends, but most are real. Girls and young women in Hollywood are willing to literally torture themselves and their bodies—surviving on juice, a few grapes, or a cracker or two for the day—just so they'll measure up (or is it measure down?) with the "right look" to help them hold onto their jobs and keep the casting agents on their side.

I've spoken with some wardrobe stylists—those men and women who fit actresses with clothing for photo shoots, parties, and awards shows—and in their most honest moments, they admit that they may be part of the problem. Here's how it works: These very talented stylists receive free clothes from various designers for celebrities to wear at events, and these free clothes are the sample sizes that models wear down the fashion runways (you know the type of body I'm talking about—think of the wafer-thin figures of Elle MacPherson, Kate Moss, and Naomi Campbell). So now these actresses are *not* being fitted to their own size, but they're trying to squeeze into a dress originally worn by a Twiggy-like model—and the actress (who may be a size 2) might get scolded because she's too heavy for the dress! Even if nothing is said, it's so embarrassing to try on a dress in front of people and have it not fit. Just think about how you feel when you're in the changing room by yourself, and now give yourself an audience!

Of course, I've worked in this culture of thinness most of my life, and it's a business where "anatomy is destiny." In just about any soap opera, or any other TV show or commercial for that matter, the dress size of the average actress is 0 or 2. These are *very* slim women! And most of them believe that if their waist is not thin enough or their body frame is not trim enough, they might lose the part they're dreaming about to a thinner-than-thou actress with the figure of Lara Flynn Boyle or the next Calista Flockhart look-alike. The press even pointed out that the female stars of long-running shows like *Friends* weighed conspicuously less during the last season that the show was on the air than the first; even the biggest stars feel pressure to downsize their bodies, no matter how spectacular they looked in their "before" photos. That's the sad shape of things in Hollywood these days.

Over the years, magazines like *People* have run stories about the almost obscene thinness among actresses in Hollywood. More recently, I've also read articles about the supposed current trend toward "healthier-looking" actresses—those who don't quite fall into the emaciated category—but the articles have used actresses like Charlize Theron as the prototype of these "normal-looking" stars. No offense to *People* or any other magazine, but in my mind, actresses like Charlize are absolutely gorgeous but also pretty darn thin. When I read articles that point to these actresses as examples of a healthier body shape in show business, my heart sinks and I find myself thinking, "If she's 'normal,' what does that make me?"

The Good Folks at Days

Before I go any further, let me make a very important point. In the midst of all of Hollywood's weight obsession, I've been spared much of this insanity, and I have the producers of *Days of Our Lives* to thank for that. Even though I've never been obese, I've also never won any awards as the thinnest actress in Hollywood. I just don't have the body type that's *ever* going to fit the mold of the "average" Hollywood actress. That's just never going to be me!

But I've been so lucky that my weight has *never* been an issue with the producers of *Days*. At times in the past, I weighed fifteen to thirty pounds more than I do today. But they never pressured me to shed some of that excess weight. They never even commented on it. The press did and mean-spirited fans did, but the producers never touched the subject. They didn't slip copies of diets under my dressing room door. They didn't send me out on forced marches to burn a few calories. From the beginning until today, my weight just hasn't been an issue with them (thank you, Ken!).

When I joined the cast of *Days*, I was a few pounds overweight but still a perfect fit for the vision the producers and writers had for Sami Brady. They said that I was a good actress, and that was what was important to them. That's why they hired me. They were bold enough to select me to play Sami, even though producers of other shows might have found me unsuitable because at the time, I weighed a little more than they would have liked. But at *Days*, my weight has always been irrelevant.

I remember one day several years ago, when I was struggling with my weight and feeling pretty bad about myself, I asked one of the executive producers if he thought I should do something about it. I wanted to know if he would have preferred that I live at a health club when I wasn't working, and whittle away at my weight. I was even considering liposuction. There was definitely a part of me that was embarrassed by being overweight, and I figured if he read me the riot act, maybe I'd finally do something about it.

Well, he couldn't have been more supportive. "Ali," he said, "I think you're beautiful, and I want you to do whatever's best for you. Your boyfriend thinks you're beautiful, doesn't he?" (This was before Dave and I got married.)

"Yes, he does."

"Then don't worry about it. You look great. And we're very happy that our show depicts beauty in all of its variety. Men don't like skeletons."

He paused for a moment, and then added, "You know, even dogs like meat on their bones."

How 'bout that! Let me tell you, that was so awesome to hear. As it turned out, I did lose some weight in the months after that conversation, but I was doing it from a place of love and support, and in the pursuit of healthy eating, not starvation. It was so much easier that way. Trust me, I'm so lucky to work for such wonderful and supportive people.

In 1997, there was an article about me in *TV Guide* proclaiming that I was "breaking all the rules." Michael Logan, the writer of that article, said that my "appeal is both surprising and encouraging," considering that one might have expected the show's producers to have hired a "reed-thin sexpot" to play the high-profile role of Sami. The article quoted *Days* head writer James Reilly as saying that my looks were an asset. "The audience identifies with Alison's young cherubic innocence," Jim was quoted as saying. "She's real, not like the anorexic, androgynous types you see in the magazines. She proves normal can be very interesting."

How cool is that?! Normal *and* interesting!

Yet even though the *Days* producers have been absolutely wonderful, I know they're the exception to the rule in Hollywood. They're in the minority on the issue of weight. Here's the cruel and ongoing reality: Most producers, directors, and casting agents usually don't hire actresses who are overweight. When I have time to audition for guest starring roles, such as on movies-of-the-week, I'd better be as lean and mean as possible if I want a shot at the role. If I (or any other actress) arrive at an audition even just five pounds heavier than what the casting director is looking for, hasta la vista, baby! There's always the pressure to be thinner. It's a constant. I wonder if it's ever going to change.

Not only do a few extra pounds reduce my chances of getting a part, but at times, casting agents have been pretty blunt in letting me know. More than once, they've told me (through my manager, or in earlier years, my mom), "Ali, can I give you a bit of advice? You should really think about losing ten or fifteen pounds." (Amazingly, they thought they were being kind and helpful! Can you believe it?!) About a year before I got the part on *Days*, when I auditioned for a role on *Beverly Hills 90210,* the casting directors politely informed me that I didn't have "the right body" for their show (by the way, after receiving that news, I comforted myself by eating—how's that for irony?!).

Of course, this Hollywood reality drives me crazy! At times, it really weighs on me (sorry—bad pun!). OK, we can agree that size and shape do matter on a show like *Baywatch*, where both men and women are parading around in a very limited amount of clothing, and their great bodies on the beach are key to the show's appeal. The same goes for an audition I went to not long ago, where the story line itself focused on the way in which weight affected the relationship between two sisters—one of whom was very thin, and the other who was heavier; obviously, the size of the actresses mattered when those roles were cast. But these are the exceptions. The plot lines of most shows don't revolve around bathing suit models who splash provocatively into the Pacific to save drowning swimmers! With most TV programs and motion pictures, it shouldn't matter whether you're ten or fifteen pounds over- or underweight. Romantic comedies, for example, would still work whether actresses weigh 105 or 140. (Remember *My Big Fat Greek Wedding?*) But, of course, don't bother arguing that case in Hollywood these days. You're wasting your breath.

The Skinny on Being Skinny

What's the logic behind the television industry's obsession with thinness? After all, there are probably many more women across America who could relate to an actress who looks real, whether she's normal-sized or even pleasantly pump—that is, someone who looks a lot more like *they* do than the actresses they usually see on TV. Take a look back through recorded history, and you'll discover that shapely and somewhat overweight women were considered beautiful (just walk through an art museum and you'll see what I mean!). So let's get real, Hollywood!

But here's the way the argument goes in show business: In most TV shows and motion pictures, there is an underlying romantic story line and a happy-ever after ending, and most viewers *don't* want to see someone who looks like them in these story lines—they want to see a fantasy of how they'd *like* life to be, including women with perfect bodies rather than more ordinary figures. (Also, don't forget about the men: Most male viewers would rather see an actress who looks like she belongs in a Victoria Secret's ad, not one who's going to Jenny Craig!)

Maybe there's some truth to that. Where are the actresses who look like average American women? Where are the models who look like real people? (Cindy Crawford, commenting on the makeup, lights, and airbrushing that are part of the modeling industry, once said that in real life, "Even I don't look like Cindy Crawford!") Sure, there are a few plump actresses on TV and in the movies, but not many (I love Camryn Manheim, don't you?—Her book, which put it right out there, was titled, *Wake Up, I'm Fat!*). I'm not so sure that the ultimate fantasy for most viewers is an actress who is bone-thin and skeletal, particularly when American women come in so many body shapes and sizes (we accept differences in hair color and eye color, but weight seems to be a completely different matter!).

One of the real ironies about weight and women in show business is that even though most casting directors I've worked with are women, they appear to be as hard or harder on actresses and their size than their male counterparts—and I just don't get it! I don't know how an entire industry can choose one body type (a very thin one) and presume that it pleases every viewer and every fan. In fact, I know it doesn't. Why can't they open their minds and choose actresses from across the spectrum—all sizes, all shapes? And anyway, I've always thought "variety is the spice of life"! Why not try casting lots of different body types for different TV shows—give people options! If they did, I think shows would attract even wider audiences than they already do.

While we're on the subject of diversity, don't get me started on the issue of aging actresses, either. Actors like Sean Connery and Harrison Ford can play leading roles for forty years, and people still love them. (I know I love them!) But youthfulness is a much bigger issue for actresses. It's such a shame that actresses like Meryl Streep and Diane Keaton sometimes have to fight for roles or create their own, despite their enormous talent. None of us stays young forever, but that doesn't make us any less interesting or talented as we grow older. We're not like gymnasts—we don't peak at eighteen!

I don't know whether things will ever change. But unless and until they do, I'd love to have you eavesdrop on some of the conversations I've had with groups of Hollywood actresses. Diet mania is not their only preoccupation, but sometimes it sure seems that way. If there's one thing actresses are good at (other than their acting ability, I hope) it's finding and exchanging diet plans with one another. When they're together, that is often Topic Number 1. So for years, I was never without a weight-loss program to replace the one that had just failed. Actresses always tell each other stories about taking one kind of weight-loss pill or another. They're sharing information on the latest exercise fad out there. Now it's even mainstream—at least in L.A., there is always talk about the newest diet fad, whether it's Dr. Atkins, Dr. Phil, the New Hollywood Diet, or whatever. At the other extreme, there are actresses I've met who keep their unusual eating (or, more accurately, noneating) behaviors to themselves, never telling a soul that they're on a near-starvation diet, or that they're binging and purging. Some of them can throw up on cue. They exercise well past the point of exhaustion. But they often keep it all hidden. It's their deep, dark secret. But guess what? Nearly everyone around them knows what's happening, particularly when their behavior becomes a little erratic. If you think it's easy to get caught up in the dieting hysteria among your own friends, just imagine what it's like in an industry where your looks are often just about the only thing that matters.

At times, I've become caught up in this rather sick preoccupation of Hollywood. A few years ago, I knew I had hit rock bottom when I actually found myself in an absolutely bizarre conversation. Another actress and I were discussing a new "diet plan" we had heard about: No, it didn't involve cutting calories or exercising more. It required dining on worms! (No, this isn't my *Fear Factor* story—that comes later.) According to the guidelines for this particular diet scheme, once these special tapeworms are in your stomach, they make themselves at home and munch away at the morsels of real food that you eat. In the process, they supposedly keep you from gaining weight! We had heard that we could eat as much as we wanted and still lose tons of weight, thanks to those hungry little worms! Luckily, the way you get them out is so gross and potentially dangerous that we were quickly turned off by the whole idea.

Sounds absolutely insane, doesn't it? And, I agree, it really is outrageous! But I have to admit that for a few brief moments, it seemed to us like something worth trying! What were we thinking?! Fortunately, we never pursued it, and my palate will be forever grateful! But when it actually sounded appealing, even for just a minute or two, I knew we were in real trouble. The sheer lunacy of the pressure to be thin can put such crazy thoughts in your head!

Chapter
11

In this chapter, let me tell you more about my own journey in the battle of the bulge. As I mentioned in the last chapter, the folks at *Days of Our Lives* have never made an issue of my weight. But that doesn't mean that I've been able to ignore it, either. I've been in show business almost all of my life, and since I've been a teenager, I've been very aware of the matter of weight and its importance in Hollywood (and throughout the entire society, for that matter). As I moved through puberty, and once my adolescent growth spurts were pretty much over, I became so busy with school and acting that I began getting less exercise than I should have. I gained a few pounds, although I know I was never really fat. But like millions of other adolescent girls, I became very self-conscious about every additional pound on the scale, particularly at this sensitive time of life where you start thinking about boys and going on dates. I also began to recognize that I couldn't eat like I did when I was ten years old; it doesn't work that way (unless, of course, you have a few friendly worms hard at work in your stomach!).

For a time, I tried a vegetarian diet, and it seemed like a healthy way to eat. But it sure didn't do much for my figure. True, I didn't eat meat, but I had pasta three or four times a week! That many carbs kept me wearing dress sizes much larger than I would have preferred. In fact, it really didn't seem to matter what kind of diet I adopted; at times, my weight would dip a few pounds, but I always gained it back. It seemed like a losing battle, and at times I became an absolute wreck! I just wanted to give up.

But then *Days of Our Lives* became part of my life. At age sixteen, I joined the show, which lifted an enormous burden from my shoulders, and let me put much less focus on the scale—or at least that's the way it should have been.

However, I've always found myself surrounded by incredibly thin actresses—and I do mean *incredibly thin*—not only on *Days* but among every other group of actresses I hung out with. As I described in Chapter 10, many, many actresses are totally absorbed with their weight, minute by minute. They feel inadequate and have their spirits absolutely crushed if they gain just a pound or two, convinced that they're fat.

When you're working with people who are so weight-conscious, it's almost inevitable that some of their obsessions rub off on you. Yes, there were (and sometimes still are) times that I wanted to be just like them. I might wake up in the morning, feel hunger pangs, have breakfast, and then become so angry with myself because I had eaten! When women in size 0 dresses would tell me very nonchalantly that they'd throw up after eating, I thought, "Maybe something's wrong with me—why am I being so moral and health-conscious about this whole thing? What's wrong with doing whatever it takes to become underweight and undersized?" I even thought at one point that a personal "weakness" was preventing me from being able to throw up my meals.

Fortunately, those thoughts didn't linger. And here's the bottom line: I know my body type and body structure, and no matter how little I eat or how much I work out, I'm never going to become the thinnest of the thin, or close to it. For better or worse, that's just not me.

OK, I will admit to the following: There was a time when I wished I had the willpower to become anorexic. I have to admit, I remember days when I felt so desperate that I tried to make myself throw up after a meal. What on earth possessed me to try it? As I wrote in Chapter 5, I remember going into the bathroom and closing the door. I sat down next to the toilet, and stuck my fingers down my throat. But nothing happened. Yes, I gagged, but I couldn't throw up. How did I feel afterward? Both disappointment and relief at the same time. Looking back, maybe someone was watching out for me—if I had been able to successfully vomit, I might have kept doing it. It could have become a way of life and spiraled way out of control. I know plenty of girls and women who have slipped into that trap. Fortunately, I found a way of growing up rather than throwing up, and I embraced a much healthier attitude about eating and body weight. But at times, it sure hasn't been easy.

Crash Diets and Other Disasters

If you're like me, you may have tried *everything* to lose weight, believing it would make you feel better about yourself. In my case, even when people would say to me, "I'd kill to have your body, Ali," I'd sometimes be thinking, "You've got to be kidding! Maybe you'd kill for Britney Spears' body—but mine?!"

Now, of course, I've matured a lot, and I'm not the maniacal dieter I used to be. I'm no longer one of those people who never met a diet she didn't like. Yet thinking back, if I had kept copies of every diet and diet book that I ever tried, they could fill up my entire garage (OK, that's an exaggeration, but not by much!). Over the years, I've gone on dozens of crash and crazy diets—none of which worked over the long term, and some of which chipped away at my overall health. I consumed low-calorie frozen entrees. I cut out snacks. I ate more fat. I ate less fat. I tried starving myself (quite literally), and then after a few days would binge on bowls of ice cream. I became one of the sweating masses crowding into trendy health clubs in Los Angeles. I exercised with several different personal trainers.

I get exhausted just thinking about all of this!

Perhaps the only approach I *didn't* try was one of those meal-replacement shake diets. You probably know the routine—drink shakes two times a day, and then have a dinner of chicken breast and vegetables, or something similar to it. I knew someone who was very overweight and actually lost eighty pounds drinking shakes. But the day he cut out the shakes and started introducing normal eating to his life again, he gained all the weight back—and more. It turned into a real nightmare for him. I knew I didn't want that to happen to me. I also knew that you can't just drink shakes for the rest of your life.

I continued to try a lot of other approaches, though. For a while, I ate custom-made meals, prepared by a nutritionist and delivered to my door. It seemed worth the effort. Well, let me tell you, the food was *so* bland (I still have this need for some salt in my diet, and there didn't seem to be *any* in this program!). The rules were very strict (I was supposed to eat particular foods in specific amounts at designated times of the day—and I became overwhelmed just trying to keep track of everything). I stuck with it for a month but just wasn't losing weight—or at least not as fast as I wanted to. At the same time, going to a restaurant was out of the question. My frustration finally boiled over. I lost my cool, canceled the delivered meals, considered myself a failure (again)—and then looked for the next diet to try!

Get the picture? If there was a diet out there I didn't try, it was only because I had placed my hope for the moment in something else. All the while—all through my teens and early twenties—my career on *Days* continued to go great. But for much of the time, I really couldn't enjoy it because I felt terrible about myself—all because of the number on the scale. For so long, I never lost any weight—certainly not in the long term—and I knew that I wasn't doing my body any good, either. The only thing that ever got thinner and frailer was my self-esteem. At times, I could talk as good a game as anyone, but during the worst times, I didn't like myself. If my weight rose, I allowed those extra pounds to undercut my self-respect and self-confidence. In short, I was making myself miserable.

Crazy, huh?

From Bad to Worse

In the past, there have been many moments when I was so tired of struggling with my weight and so frustrated with

Hollywood's vision of perfection that I was at the breaking point! I felt like throwing up my hands and throwing in the towel on show business. That's how deep my despair had gotten. Of course, for my entire life, acting has been my dream. It's what I love. It's what I'm good at. But I admit that sometimes the "weight thing" really got to me.

More than once my self-loathing overheated, and I would absolutely lose it. At the mall, I might try on a cute outfit and feel that it looked absolutely terrible on me, or that it just didn't fit the way I thought it should. Or I would peruse pictures taken of me at a photo shoot, and when I appeared heavy in my own eyes, my unhappiness and misery would boil over. I'd curse myself for not having willpower. I'd have a full-blown meltdown. You get the point, right? It could be pretty ugly.

I remember a few incidents that I'm almost embarrassed to tell you about. Several times, I stormed into my kitchen, sobbing uncontrollably, and cleaned nearly everything out of my refrigerator and cupboards. The sugar-rich soft drinks went first . . . then the Haagen-Dazs bars . . . the lemonade mix . . . the sugary cereals. I tossed every "unhealthy" or high-calorie food within reach into a large trash bag, or even worse, I'd occasionally fling it against the wall and watch it land in a heap on the floor (Yes, I was a cleaning lady's worst nightmare!). Eventually, once the trash bag was filled to overflowing, I'd drag it out to the garbage bin, with tears rolling down my cheeks. Can you imagine what that scene was like? Definitely a pitiful sight. When it was all over, after calming down a bit, I'd go to the market and fill up my shopping cart with items from the health-food aisle there was nothing with sugar, and certainly nothing that tasted good—and I'd start the next diet, but I'd do it from a very negative, very unhappy place. Inevitably, of course, I'd fail on that one, too, usually ending up by going out and having the dessert that I had been craving for weeks.

This agonizing cycle repeated itself, again and again.

The Fans Weigh In

In the midst of all this craziness, I used to get my share of fan letters from *Days'* viewers who said they had noticed that I had gained five or ten pounds and were determined to tell me what I should be doing about it. Most of them tried to be helpful. Some tucked a diet and a few recipes into the envelope. On occasion, however, their comments were pretty surprising. A few actually came right out and told me how "fat and ugly" I was! (Give me a break!) Or that I'd "look better if you'd just stop eating!" One letter writer said, "You fat cow, leave Austin alone!" (Can you believe somebody would sit down and take the time to write out and actually mail something like that?!) If that wasn't enough, one "fan" threw in a comment that I was "a terrible actress," too. No one ever included a Weight Watchers gift certificate along with their letter, but there sure have been some nasty messages over the years.

Fortunately, most of my fan mail is *very* positive. People write and ask all kinds of questions about the show. They love (or they hate) Sami. They describe in great detail what Sami should have done in certain story lines on the show. Or they'll ask me what some of the other cast members are really like. If the subject gets around to weight, most of the comments are very supportive. I weigh less today than I did in my earlier years on the show, and when fans write letters, attend *Days* events, or stop me in shopping malls, a common opening line—and it's a positive one—is, "Ali, you've lost so much weight!" I want to thank every one of you who has supported me that way. But even though only a small minority of the letters and statements are critical, they sure do get your attention! Particularly when I was younger, and would read some of the mean-spirited things people would occasionally write in chat rooms, for example, it really hurt, and sometimes it would even make me cry! When you're fighting your own internal demons, it's hard to have someone egg you on or attack you that way—it's just not helpful or comforting. If I took them seriously, they could ruin my whole day—or more! (By the way, I remember when Bryan Dattilo and some of my other costars showed me some of their "hate mail," and I realized it wasn't just me that fans picked on now and then.) I finally understood the following: You just can't please everyone all the time—particularly when some viewers already don't like you because you're playing a villain!

These days, people still occasionally come up to me on the street and say something like, "I'm so glad you stopped eating so much; you didn't look all that great before!"—and they mean it! Or they'll say, "Ali, you look so much better than you used to!" I actually think most people are trying to be complimentary, so that's the way I take it. What's the point of driving yourself crazy over it?

I've also been strengthened by comments from fans who have described their own battles with weight. Of course, I've known all along that I've never been alone in this struggle, sharing it not only with my acting peers, but also with millions of girls and women everywhere. When I read the statistics that about *fifty million Americans* are by definition overweight or obese, it's very alarming. Too many Americans are ballooning to perilous proportions, which can undermine their self-esteem, trigger depression, and ruin their physical health. Yet my own mail brings the statistics down to a personal level: So many people are so concerned with the way they look, and they're constantly dieting or at least thinking about it.

It seems that so many issues in women's lives—whether it's relationships with men, insecurities about their appearance, even cattiness toward other women—frequently lead back to weight. As girls and women tell me in their letters, the scale is a powerful force that has a grip on how they feel about themselves and relate to the world around them. That's the way our culture seems to work. Like the actresses I described earlier, ever so many overweight people are trying to become thin, and skinny people are trying to become even skinnier. From my own experience, I know it starts in adolescence or even earlier (a Harris poll showed that one-third of girls ages ten to twelve described themselves as overweight!). In high school, some girls are already taking diet pills and exercising to the point of collapse. And the fashions of the day—including the low-riding jeans and the tight, truncated tank tops—certainly don't help, do they? They reveal tummies that (unless you're one of the chosen few) require hours of sweating and straining in the gym to look "just right."

As you can tell, I have moments of absolute frustration when it comes to the topic of weight. In fact, one of my motivations for writing about this issue grew out of a trip I made to a pizza parlor a few years ago, accompanied by a friend and his younger sister who was eight years old at the time. This young girl sat at a table with six other eight-year-olds, and I remember one of them saying, "We can't eat any bread because it's too fattening!" That's a pretty startling statement, particularly considering that all of these kids were rail-thin! I recall thinking, "There's something terribly wrong here."

I decided that because of my high visibility as an actress, maybe I could help bring some sensibility to this issue. I knew I didn't want to write a diet book, but more than anything else, this section of the book is intended to raise my readers' awareness. That's what you'll find in the pages that follow.

Chapter 12

After years of waging war on my own body, I have a much more positive perspective on diets and weight—and, yes, even on life in general. I've gone through several generations of diets to get to where I am today. But finally, I'm at a place where I want to be. I've been able to stay at a weight that I'm happy with, and most of the stress surrounding eating is gone. I'm going to tell you more about my own journey, but *not* because I want you to start eating like I do (as a matter of fact, I really don't follow a formal diet plan anymore, and perhaps there's no need for you to do so, either). But you might find my own path interesting and even inspiring. Again, this is *not* a diet book with an eating plan that I'm recommending. One thing I'm sure of is that no diet program is right for everyone; what I've learned is that each person is going to have to find the diet or health plan that fits him or her best.

Although I had been preoccupied with my weight for years, my journey toward a much healthier lifestyle actually began in 1998. I had been on *Days of Our Lives* for about five years, and although my career couldn't have been going any better, my battle with the scale was sometimes an absolute disaster.

For me, the change began one afternoon when I paid a visit to Dr. Jay, my dentist (I've changed his name to protect his privacy). I was there for a routine cleaning and examination. But as Dr. Jay peered into my mouth, a startled expression came over his face.

"Ali, I see a cavity." It wasn't the news I wanted to hear, but it wasn't the end of the world, either.

Then Dr. Jay added, "What's with all this sugar you've been eating?"

Sugar?! I had no idea what he was talking about. I tried to keep my cool, and I pleaded my case.

"Jay, I really do eat a healthy diet," I said. "I don't eat very much sugar or anything else that's bad for me. And I brush all the time."

Dr. Jay raised a skeptical eyebrow.

"Ali, your teeth aren't lying to me. You have a cavity. You're eating sugar. Now, tell me what you eat."

I was really getting annoyed. Growing up, I was lucky that my mom didn't believe in keeping a lot of sugar-laden snacks or sugar-rich cereals around the house; fruit was our primary snack. But I have to admit: When my mom wasn't looking, my brothers and I would sneak sugary cereals into the house and hide them. (Sorry, Mom!) So I did develop an appetite for sugar, although my mom certainly had nothing to do with it. And I guess those cravings never really waned as I entered adulthood.

I started to answer Dr. Jay's question.

"OK, I drink one or two Cokes a day."

"Oh, really. Ali, that's *all* sugar. What else?"

Geez, he was getting a little confrontational, and maybe I was becoming a bit defensive.

"I love pasta, so I eat it quite often," I told him. "Maybe three times a week."

"Pasta, huh? Ali, no wonder you're a little puffy."

Puffy!! I had heard a lot of words to describe my excess pounds, but never "puffy!"

I continued to list other foods that I ate regularly. But as I mentioned each of them, one after another, I gradually began to feel this sinking sensation. "Oh, no," I thought to myself. "Maybe my diet isn't so healthy after all."

That was the truth. I wasn't coming close to a sugar-free diet. I ate desserts much too often. I loved breakfast cereals that were "honey flavored." I ate bread, showing little restraint whenever it was on the table.

You get the drift. I felt a little stunned and pretty embarrassed.

Dr. Jay finally said, "Ali, let me tell you how I live my life."

He sat down and began to describe how he had eaten for years. In supermarkets, he spent most of his time in the outer aisles, filling his shopping cart with foods like fresh fruits and vegetables (so it certainly wasn't an Atkins-type program). For breakfast, he had a very low carbohydrate cereal. Later in the day, he ate modest amounts of high-quality, high-protein meats (so it sure wasn't an Ornish-like plan); for a typical lunch, he ate a salad with slices of chicken breast in it. Throughout the day, he kept his intake of carbohydrates well under control. No baked potatoes. No side orders of rice or pasta.

"What about the four basic food groups?" I asked him.

"Forget about them!" he said emphatically. "My approach keeps me fit and healthy. I think the food groups are obsolete."

"And what about losing weight? That's what I'm really interested in."

"You might lose some weight on this type of program," he said. "But you should be less interested in weight loss and more interested in being healthy. If you adopt a healthy diet, the weight will take care of itself."

Despite all the diets I had been on, much of what Dr. Jay was saying made sense. He wasn't talking about a fanatical program that leaves your stomach growling from daybreak 'til bedtime. He wasn't feeding himself only fruit before noon, or gorging on rice after 6 P.M. He wasn't gulping down a cupboard-full of meal-replacement drinks. He wasn't weighing his food or keeping track of every last calorie.

Dr. Jay also talked about following a program for life. That's right—a *lifetime* commitment! (That sure took my breath away for a few moments; I was much more accustomed to going on a crash diet, following it hard-core for three or four weeks, and then being done with it and going back to my old way of eating!) Dr. Jay's approach was so different than the crazy diets I'd been on for so many years.

"Ali, the way you've been eating is not how you should treat your body," Dr. Jay told me. "Maybe my approach isn't right for you. But find a plan that works for you, and stick with it for the long term."

I have to admit, Dr. Jay was a walking advertisement for his own program. He was trim and fit, and he told me about female patients who had been overweight, had started eating like he does, and looked fantastic. One of them, he said, had been more than twenty pounds overweight and a year after adopting the program, she posed for *Playboy*! Now that's what I call a transformation! As he told me her story, there was a part of me thinking, "Sign me up—I'll do it!" But more than anything, he sent me out into the world with something to think about.

"Is there a book I can read that describes your diet?" I asked.

"No, the books out there are too intense in terms of playing havoc with your blood sugar. So you can take a few tips from me, but experiment a little, too. Create a program that's right for your own body. You can do it."

Time for a Change

I drove home (with a numb jaw!) thinking about Dr. Jay's advice. Was he right? . . . Could he have found something that might work for me, too? . . . Or could it at least point me in the right direction? Could I create my own way of eating that would put me on a healthier path and keep me there?

Yes, Dr. Jay was truly inspiring. But, let's get real, Ali— I had failed on every other diet I had ever tried. So why would this one be any different?

Later that day, I told Dave (then my boyfriend, now my husband) about my conversation with Dr. Jay. I complained about my weight (as usual). I lamented that I had never found a diet that worked. You should have heard me—it was a classic case of whining! Dave let me ramble on for a few minutes; it certainly wasn't the first time that

(Author's personal collection)

Enjoying the sunny
Mexican beach
with Dave

I had griped to him about my weight, and it was a real pity party this time! But after I had my say, he jumped in with a different reaction than I had been used to hearing. In fact, he gave me some food for thought (no pun intended!) and offered a suggestion.

"Ali, I've told you so many times that I love you no matter what you weigh. I think you're absolutely beautiful just the way you are." So far, so good. "But, Ali, you complain about your weight *all the time!* You're a go-getter in every other aspect of your life, but not this one. You go after your dreams and what you want in life, but not when it comes to your weight. Why is that?"

Before I could answer, Dave continued. "Decide what

you want to do, take action, and stop complaining about it. Don't gripe all the time but do nothing about it!"

Wow.

That was tough for me to hear. In essence, Dave was saying, "Put up or shut up!"

I was silent for a few seconds. I realized that Dave was right. I had always gone after everything I wanted in life—except a thinner body. I had a mental block against committing to any dietary program. No wonder I hadn't succeeded.

There was an awkward pause.

"You're right, Dave," I finally told him.

For the rest of the day—and the rest of the week, for that matter—I did a lot of thinking. I came face-to-face with the reality of how I had approached dieting for years. I admitted to myself that I had been in denial about so many things, from the effect of drinking two or three sugar-laden Cokes a day to the bread that I enjoyed with so many meals. (It's amazing how you can con yourself into believing that your diet is approaching perfection when it's lacking in so many areas.) I realized that if I could apply the same hard work and the same commitment—and show the same resilience—that I did for everything else, maybe I could finally succeed in losing weight. As the days passed, I really began to believe it.

A New Life

Knowing how to eat is 200 percent of the battle. And it's not an exaggeration to say that I embarked on an entirely new way of life. Seriously! Beginning in February 1999, I adopted some of what Dr. Jay had told me, and I changed other components of his eating plan—sometimes choosing different foods and doing some other fine-tuning along the way. But one thing was certain: I became hard-core about cutting sugar (my big weakness) out of my diet. Completely.

Today, I keep an eye on the amount of carbohydrates I eat, but there are no hard-and-fast rules that (in the past) always ended up being broken. The days of trying to eat zero carbs and zero sugar are gone. In fact, I'm very flexible and relaxed—no rigid rules and no concrete eating plan, but rather some general directions that I'm taking. No crazy diets because you can't live on shakes or pineapple all your life—and they'll throw your metabolism into a tailspin! No fad foods because you'll get sick of them in no time! And I certainly don't count calories (yuck!) or keep a daily food diary. If I tried to stick to some strict, unbending rules, I know I couldn't follow them for a lifetime, and I'd make myself miserable.

Once I changed my primary goal from being superthin to being superhealthy—and once I stopped bashing myself and hating myself because of what the scale said—I lost a lot of weight. That's really what happened.

As I write these words, it's been over four years now, and I'm not looking back. I've lost close to thirty pounds from my peak weight—yes, thirty pounds!—and thank goodness, I've been able to maintain that weight loss (although it's always a challenge to stay there!).

Initially, as those pounds came off, I remember Dave telling me that my blue jeans were hanging on me. "You look like a gangster," he teased me. "You need to buy a new pair."

He was right, and I went shopping for jeans at The Gap, and bought a few pair with a better fit (size 8, if I remember correctly). But then I lost another eight or nine pounds, and even the new jeans were literally around my hips! Dave took one look and said, "Ali, haven't you had time to get those new jeans?"

"I did! These *are* my new jeans."

So I went shopping again, and brought home size 4. It was crazy—I was living every dieter's dream of being forced to buy a new wardrobe! As the pounds came off, I felt so much better about myself. I felt healthier, too. It was so inspiring and so motivating. And when the size 4's started to fit a little loose on me—well, I knew I was doing something right.

The Fans React

When I lost all that weight, people took notice. I remember Corina Duran, one of our makeup artists at *Days*, teasing me when I showed up one day wearing a baggy denim jail shirt. (Sami was on Death Row, remember?) She exclaimed, "Ali, how dare you hide your stomach under that big shirt! You look great—you have to show it off!"

So the next day, I arrived on the set with a fitted button-down top that I had tied at my waist. And what was Corina's reaction? She looked at me and said, "Now, you're just showing off!"

Positive comments like that—and the weight that I had successfully lost—were motivating. My strengthened will-power came from my new look and those glances in the

(Theo & Juliet Photography/Zelf-Fridtzius)

After slimming
down

mirror that had me saying, "Geez, I have to go shopping and buy smaller-sized clothes!"

Meanwhile, viewers of *Days* noticed the change, too, and I was deluged with hundreds of letters and e-mails, with fans asking how I had slimmed down. Here's what one fan wrote:

Alison, I envy your determination and inner strength to become healthy and live a healthier life. That determination is something I've had trouble hanging onto. All my life, I've been referred to as the 'chunky one.' Even my family doctor would poke fun at my weight sometimes (which REALLY got my spirits down).

Even though no one ever called me 'fat' (at least not to my face), I have always seen myself as fat. The fact that I'm 22 years old, and still can't shed what my parents politely call my 'baby fat,' is pretty discouraging. I have tried almost every diet out there, and haven't found one with lasting results once you stop the plan.

I was floored (and jealous and envious) one day when I was watching Days of Our Lives, *and you walked out in this flattering dress, and I realized just how much weight you have actually lost and how fit you looked. I've been curious about your dieting plan ever since.*

I enthusiastically agree with the natural and healthy path you've chosen to assist you in your weight loss and your quest to be healthier. I feel confident that the same path will work for me and a lot of other health-challenged people out there. I would greatly appreciate any feedback or advice you might have for me.

Linda

When I make public appearances at *Days'* events, some fans want to talk about my weight and not much else (even if my eating habits are no longer my own obsession, someone somewhere seems obsessed with them!). When magazines have run articles about how I lost fifteen or twenty or twenty-five pounds, or *Entertainment Tonight* and *E! Entertainment* have documented my dieting efforts, readers have certainly responded, and I've received sacks of letters about it. Most of it has been very positive. There have been plenty of letters from people who told me that

(Author's personal collection)

Posing on the red carpet!

they've been motivated by my own success. Many have cheered me on. Or they've thanked me for publicly acknowledging that the battle to lose weight isn't an easy one. They've described their own struggles, their own successes and their own failures:

Hello Alison—I read your article in Soap Opera Digest *regarding sugar. As an experiment, I decided to give up granulated sugar. Not only did I lose 27 pounds, but I also lost any desire to ever eat sugar again. I went from a size 12–14 to a svelte size 6 (now I'm quoting my husband!). I found that I also crave more protein than carbohydrates and my energy level has soared. So THANK YOU for the interview which inspired me to follow in your footsteps.*

Gail

Hi. I have been a Days *fan for many years, and my daughter Brit started watching with me last year. She took a liking to you immediately. Any time I buy* Soap Opera Digest, *we look for articles about you.*

When we began to notice your weight loss, Brit thought you were losing like other actresses who had become way too skinny. Then we read an article about you talking about your weight loss. When Brit read what you said about being responsible and how you did it for yourself and only you, she was very impressed.

As we read more articles, and learned that you weren't obsessive about your weight, she began to have double doubts about what her friends had to say about weight and how they were so preoccupied with it. She started to realize that you were happy with yourself no matter what. She very rarely mentions her weight anymore, and the credit goes to you.

I just want to thank you for being such an inspiration. Good luck to you in your career, and I hope all your dreams come true.

Molly

Chapter 13

These days, the way I eat is constantly a work in progress. It's certainly different today than my diet of four years ago, or even four months ago. My own diet plan (I think of it more as a "lifestyle") is constantly changing, forever evolving, always fluid. I don't think of myself as dieting, but rather as eating right for myself.

I've managed to gain some insights with age (I'm all of twenty-six as I write these words!), and I've recognized that feeling great is definitely more important to me than achieving ultrathinness. Sure, I still have bad days when perhaps I overdo it. But if something doesn't seem to be working for a while, I'm not married to it—sometimes I make changes and try new foods and approaches, meal by meal. It makes the process much more interesting.

As I already mentioned, I've never had the intention of turning this into a diet book and recommending a specific program that I think you and everyone else should adopt. I know better than to think that I have the expertise to

counsel you on the diet that's best for you. I'm not a nutritionist, and I don't know what appeals to your palette, nor
am I a doctor who understands what's optimal for your
own body and well-being. You certainly know best what
might work for you, and what it may take for you to stick
with it for the long term. If you want to try the latest diet
fad, go ahead, but don't allow yourself to be brought
down if it doesn't work. More than anything, I want to encourage you to eat a healthy diet, and the rest will probably fall into place.

Now, please don't misunderstand me: I don't approach
my eating lackadaisically. I do carefully consider what goes
onto my plate every single meal. But it's not an obsession. I
try to use good judgment, making sure my meals support
my goals, while never being fanatical about it or latching
onto gimmicks. Whenever I've tried to follow a strict program, I've ended up eventually cheating, and then feeling
angry and resentful that I had tried the diet in the first place.

In this chapter, let me tell you about a few of my own
approaches that I've used in recent times when planning
my meals and snacks. They may make sense to you—or
maybe they won't. But perhaps if you take a little of what
I do, and borrow some other dietary strategies from
friends, family members, or other books, you might find
yourself creating your own plan that's the perfect fit.
Remember, this is how *I* often eat, but I don't pretend to
have the answers for you. If you want to try some of my
lifestyle changes, great—but you might find other ideas
that work much better for you:

- I shop completely differently than I once did. It fact, a
  trip to the supermarket can turn into something of an

adventure these days. Years ago, Dr. Jay told me to read food labels more carefully, and I was surprised at just how much information is there. Just an example or two: Breakfast cereals can differ considerably in the amount of sugar they have (some cereals not only list sugar as a major ingredient, but corn syrup and honey aren't far behind!). One brand of wheat bread that I used to buy has corn syrup as its second ingredient!

- I eat breakfast every day. Not only is it important for me to start off the morning right, but on the *Days* set, you never know when you're going to get a break to eat—you can be on stage for hours and never have a moment to grab a bite, and you better be ready to perform the most demanding scenes at 9 or 10 or 11 A.M., if that's what the schedule calls for! For breakfast, I often have Puffed Wheat these days. Or I'll prepare an egg omelet, making it interesting by adding chives and basil from my garden, and perhaps a little cilantro or cheese. Or I'll eat an egg sandwich made with one slice of whole wheat bread, a little cheese, and turkey bacon. And by the way, if there's a particular brand of breakfast cereal that I don't eat very often—but I'm just dying to have it—I will! I'm not going to be driven crazy by my diet, and I'm not going to let it keep me from enjoying life!

- For lunch, a typical meal might be an open-faced tuna salad sandwich, prepared on a piece of bread. Or I might make a salad with plenty of lettuce, other vegetables, and chicken breast. I'll often chop up and toss all kinds of things into the salad bowl—apples, chives, turkey bacon, shredded turkey, or a little cheese. I try to add a healthy carb like a yam or brown rice at lunch to help me get through the rest of the day.

- For dinner, I usually have some protein—perhaps a modest serving of meat, chicken, or fish (salmon is one of my favorites!). I minimize the carbs I have in the evening, which reduces the likelihood of my blood sugar levels going haywire. In the evenings, I'm also likely to avoid all carb foods like corn, potatoes, pasta, rice, and bread, but I'll have some vegetables like broccoli or green beans. Variety is key, and I don't overrely on any single food or food group—or deprive myself completely of anything, either.

- In general, no matter what meal we're talking about, I lean a little more toward protein than carbohydrates when thinking about what to eat; when I do, fat storage becomes less of a problem for me. Protein also seems to curb my appetite better than other types of food. So I eat modest portions of high-quality, high-protein fish and chicken. And if I have a pasta salad for lunch one day, I make a mental note to take it easy on the carbs the next day. Sensible, but not fanatical.

- I eat plenty of fresh produce. I realize that I need some fruits and vegetables since, without enough complex carbohydrates, I may be playing havoc with my blood sugar levels. I might have an orange in the morning, for example, which doesn't have the high concentration of sugar as a glass of orange juice (I remember reading that juice provides the equivalent of the sugar in eight oranges, but an actual piece of fruit has a much more modest amount of sugar, and tends to fill me up). In the supermarket, my shopping cart may have vegetables like bell peppers in it (I love their flavor, texture, and color). And I'm always trying new foods to cook with—I used leeks in my omelet the other day . . . delicious!

- I spend a lot of time in my dressing room at NBC, waiting to be called to the *Days* set. While it might be tempting to take advantage of the candy and bagels available for the cast and crew, I rarely let that temptation get to me anymore. Sure, the crew works very hard, they're on their feet all day, and they want something substantial for lunch or dinner, so the show's producers make sure they're well fed. But as an alternative, I rely on my own healthy snacks, often stopping at the deli on the way to the studio for some cold cuts (like turkey pastrami or smoked turkey). When I get hungry, I'll raid the refrigerator in my dressing room, roll up some turkey, often using iceberg lettuce as my "bread," and perhaps make them a little more interesting with some Muenster cheese and avocado. Or I might have a healthy snack of celery with a little peanut butter or seasoning salt.

- There are some foods that I eat less often (as far as I'm concerned, no food is taboo, but there are some that I try not to do to excess). Pizza isn't something I overdo. I've reduced the amount of starchy foods I eat. I've cut down on bread and other heavy foods. The same with refined sugar; at one point early in the process, I eliminated sugar from my diet completely— cold turkey—tossing out the Cokes in my refrigerator (I even gave up my beloved Diet Cokes for a while!), and replacing them with iced tea (with a little fruit water, but no other sweetener). After drinking two or three sugar-saturated soft drinks a day for years, I found that in just a couple weeks, I lost the compulsion to reach for something sweet. I put my sweet tooth to rest. These days, I drink a Diet Coke from time to time, but not in excess. Some people, however, can't stop consuming sugar on a dime, particularly when you're talking about something they've been eating all their life; maybe you need to wean yourself gradually from sugar-laden foods, which is fine. Do whatever works best for you. But, let me tell you, after a while your sugar cravings *will* subside. That's why I even cut out the Nutra-Sweet, too. You have to get your taste buds off the sugar cravings! So if you really cut all sugar and sugar substitutes, eventually sugary sodas and the related stuff aren't particularly appealing.

- I've dramatically reduced my dependence on coffee. For much of my life, I was so hooked on caffeine that I used to salivate just driving by a Starbucks (you're right—that's a bit of an exaggeration!). But once I weaned myself from coffee and switched instead to iced tea or Ice Blended, I could barely stand the smell or the taste of coffee anymore. The acidity of the bean almost made me ill. As for caffeine, I try to keep the lid on the number of caffeine-spiked diet sodas I consume, which required a real change in mindset. There was a time when my closest friends would give me cases of Diet Cokes as birthday presents! I remember once getting a Coca-Cola lap blanket as a gift. But I now rely on much healthier drinks (although the lap blanket has survived my decision to rid the house of most soft-drink reminders!).

- Now, let me be honest: I still love desserts, and I eat

them from time to time. But I don't have them—and
certainly don't feel I need them—every day. I remember times when I've been on vacation, and I ended up
at some restaurant, and rationalized it this way: "Hey,
I'm on vacation—and when am I ever going to come
back to this restaurant? So I'll splurge and enjoy myself." Nothing's wrong with that—but I also know
that if I have a few cookies four or five nights in a row
(which I very rarely do!), I better get back on track
once I get home. I also try to choose desserts that I really enjoy (candy bars aren't my thing, so when I'm
selecting desserts, I make sure it's something I truly
love!). Not long ago, when *US Weekly* did an interview with me and featured my weight loss, I wasn't
the least bit hesitant to tell them that I had recently
joined some girlfriends for a big dinner at Emeril's in
Las Vegas. Why not?! It's all a matter of give and
take, appreciating the good things that make life enjoyable, while never losing sight of the overall goal of
maintaining my weight at a certain level.

- My advice to my friends (and maybe it will make
  sense to you as well) is that if you absolutely crave
  something—let's say a slice of cheesecake, for example—you might as well have the cheesecake (a small
  slice, of course!) and be done with it, rather than feeling deprived and obsessing about it. In my own case, I
  won't go through life completely avoiding chocolate
  cake; and if my mom (who is a wonderful baker!)
  makes a special dessert (like blueberry pie!), I'm the
  first in line.

  I've known people who are just dying to eat a cookie,
  but have convinced themselves that they shouldn't—

so instead they'll have a slice of bread, and when that doesn't satisfy them, they'll end up eating an entire bag of baby carrots with peanut butter (I know this from personal experience!) and maybe a soda or two. Before all is said and done, they've eaten eight or nine different food items in lieu of the cookie—but then they'll probably end up eating the cookie anyway! My philosophy: If you're feeling deprived, you're going to fall off the wagon at some point. So keep the portions of desserts relatively small, give yourself a little latitude, and *enjoy life!*

- I carry a water bottle with me nearly all the time. Water helps control my appetite, so I drink it all day long. If you're accustomed to eating and snacking throughout the day, water will help quench your appetite and keep you from reaching for food as often.

- I used to eat when I was bored or anxious, and there are plenty of tedious times at the studio when you're waiting (and waiting and waiting) to be called to the set for rehearsals or to shoot your scenes. In the past, there were times when I'd pace my dressing room, wondering what I could eat. When that would happen, I'd often break the tedium by walking to the vending machines, and buy a bag of potato chips, a candy bar, or a soda—just because I was bored, not because my stomach was growling! It became a huge problem for me—and it threatened to make *me* huge as well! So I've worked hard on eating only when I'm hungry. I've found other ways to cut the stress and shatter the boredom that used to lead me to food. I always keep my mind occupied—by answering fan mail or e-mail, for example, or surfing the net. I listen to classical music, sometimes with the lights dimmed and a burning candle nearby (I grew up in a household where my mom played classical violin, and the kids always played one instrument or another). Also, I occupy my time by talking with fellow actors or doing all kinds of absolutely crazy things—I actually taught myself to juggle, if you can believe that!

Even though these are general guidelines that I've often used, let me stress again that my diet is fluid and constantly changing. I've gone through phases where I feel like eating carrots and not much of anything else. Or there have been times when the sight of a hamburger almost turns my stomach, and I can't go near it. I've become very good at "going with the flow," and adapting to whatever works at the moment. If this sounds like a comfortable approach, maybe a rigid diet isn't for you, either. At the same time, I know that I'm in a "rest-of-my-life" situation—I'll never go back to eating (or overeating) the way I used to. It's given me a real sense of "diet liberation."

What About Portion Size?

I realized a while ago that we don't need as much food to sustain us as we often consume. It's just like sleep . . . your body may need only five or six hours a night, but people who are accustomed to getting seven or eight hours feel deprived if they sleep less. So my own portion sizes rarely get out of control—I'm very careful not to overdo it. (Listen up! This is a real key to my success with weight management!)

Our society is obsessed with supersized portions, apparently as a way to "get more for our money" at restaurants. But our bodies don't require that much fuel. Our pasta bowls don't need to be filled to overflowing. We aren't supposed to make every meal a Thanksgiving feast, 365 days a year. I simply don't eat as much as I used to, and because my stomach and my appetite have shrunk with time, I really don't miss overindulging.

At the same time, however, as I've already written, I won't deprive myself, either. If I really feel like eating pasta, I'll have it—but I don't need a Herculean-sized bowl of pasta to feel satisfied. I'm content just having a side-dish-sized portion and not getting carried away—I simply don't need a second or third helping, and I feel quite satisfied without them.

When eating in restaurants, I don't let myself get so caught up in social conversation that I eat unconsciously. Let me tell you what works for me in restaurants: I often order both an appetizer and an entrée, allowing myself to indulge in as many different tastes as possible. So I may order an appetizer such as capreza (sliced tomatoes, Mozzarella cheese, fresh basil); it's a completely different taste than the chicken and the vegetables that I may have for an entrée. Or I'll have a salad for an appetizer, and then salmon and broccoli as the main dish. I'll leave some of each on my plate, and take the leftovers home for the following day. It's a great way to dine. And when I eat this way, I'm not hungry when I leave the restaurant—but I'm not stuffed, either.

I also don't obsess over what I'm eating; when I was completely preoccupied with the food I put on my plate, I remember having internal debates with myself over whether or not I should take another bite. I'd feel terrible about myself if I ate more than I had planned. What a horrible way to live! If I ate something that wasn't part of my "perfect" program, it chipped away at my self-esteem. For me, that was the hardest part of being on a formal diet— every time I slipped, I'd beat myself up over it, convinced that something was wrong with me. Today, however, balance is what I'm seeking and I usually find it. Gradually, I began to see beyond the scale and started to trust my gut instincts about who I really am, what's really important, and how much I should eat.

What's Cooking?

Now, what about time in the kitchen? Well, I'm no Emeril or Julia Child. I don't ever expect to be, either, and I guess I'm a latecomer to the art of creating culinary masterpieces.

When I was nineteen years old, I got my first apartment and my introduction to dabbling in my own kitchen. As comfortable as I had been living with my parents, I was feeling a little crowded at home and decided to become Ms. Independent! Most of my friends had already gone off to college and were living in dorm rooms, and my parents thought it was fine for me to get out on my own. So I bought a bed, a beautiful Laura Ashley comforter, and some wicker furniture, and I borrowed a coffee table from my parents' house. And, of course, then I had to deal with the kitchen.

Well, some of my earliest efforts—even the simplest ones—were an absolute disaster! Let me tell you about the time I ruined a bag of microwave popcorn! Now really, how hard can it be to pop some popcorn? Yet, apparently it required far more talent than I could muster at that moment. As I recall, the instructions on the bag called for setting the microwave oven at two minutes. But that wasn't good enough for me. I made the executive decision that two minutes just didn't seem right. So I set it at five minutes, and let her rip!

Well, before I knew it, the bag of popcorn had actually exploded! And then it burst into flames! Can you believe it—I started a fire in my own microwave oven! Quite clever, don't you think?!

Fortunately, I'm happy to report that my culinary talents have taken a turn for the better. In fact, I've actually become pretty good at a growing number of dishes. But I've also learned a few lessons—for example, you really have to pay attention! I remember one evening when I was preparing spaghetti with a really yummy mushroom cream sauce that my mom had made. Well, it's really not very complicated to make spaghetti, right? Yet I somehow turned the cooking experience into a wild event that soon resembled an E-ticket ride at Disneyland. Here's what happened: I put the spaghetti in a pot, and when the water started boiling, I turned the flame down a bit. So far, so good. But then I went into the living room and began watching *Seinfeld*. Big mistake! Thirty minutes later when the show was finally over, I returned to the kitchen—and was greeted by a torrent of water that might have posed a challenge for a seasoned river rafter! What a mess! The lesson: Don't let yourself become distracted (even by *Seinfeld*!) when there's something cooking on the stove!

As you can tell, I started from literally nowhere, ruined

quite a few meals (and caused a flash flood or two), but today, I *love* being in the kitchen—and I'm getting better all the time! I learned a lot by watching the Food Channel, and chefs like Emeril Lagasse convinced me that cooking was something that I could do. He makes it sound so easy, doesn't he? And he makes it fun, too, which is a great way to approach just about everything in life. Many of my meal and dessert creations aren't half bad. (I can also proudly proclaim that I make a pretty mean—and fire-free—microwave popcorn these days, too!) When I eat at restaurants and give instructions to waiters on how I'd like my meal prepared, I often get a rather boring and tasteless dish. But in my own kitchen, I've become creative with spices and herbs, including some from my own herb garden. I love to experiment and try new dishes. I have a great time being inventive—for example, making a chicken dish by sautéing it lightly for flavor (showing some restraint with the oil), then baking it, and finally bringing on the herbs, starting with garlic and rosemary. Take my word for it, the taste can be pretty amazing! Or if I'm in the mood for a Mexican-themed dinner, I might simmer the chicken, mix in some cilantro, and then use it in a stew (rather than serving it with tortillas).

I sometimes adapt recipes from magazines like *Bon Apetite* and *Gourmet* so they're more to my liking. Or I'll actually combine two recipes—for example, a pasta dish plus a tomato chicken sauce. I'll take the sauce and make it thicker by adding artichoke hearts and broccoli. (I call it my "chicken sink stew," because I'll add any and every vegetable that's in my refrigerator and turn the sauce into a chunky delight! Then I'll prepare the pasta, too (for my husband Dave), although I'll often eat only the stew myself.

I've also enjoyed a bonus that comes with cooking: When I prepare a meal, I'm not as hungry once I sit down at the dining room table. (Does that happen to you?) Maybe I've spent so much time smelling the food in the kitchen that it starts filling me up—at least it seems that way. Cooking is a great stress reliever for me, too, because it keeps my mind focused on following the recipe, measuring ingredients, and so on. It almost becomes something like a meditation. Whatever the explanation, I don't eat as much when I cook, compared to when someone else does the work in the kitchen.

Even though I don't overindulge in treats like cookies, I love baking them for Dave—and so I won't be tempted to overindulge myself, I might put nuts in them (that's because I hate nuts!). I'm not even tempted when I've "doctored" the cookies that way (although I must admit that peanut butter cookies sure can whet my appetite!).

Dave is great when it comes to my cooking. He has inspired me to become very adventurous in the kitchen, and usually likes whatever I whip up (at least that's what he tells me). Of course, he and I also love eating together, and—here's the best part—he often cleans up the kitchen afterward. He says that since I've worked so hard to prepare the meal, the least he can do is wash the dishes. What a sweetheart!

A Little Perspective

As you can tell, I've done a lot of thinking about food, diets, and weight in the last few years. I see so many of my fellow actresses torture themselves over what they should and shouldn't eat. But I've had the luck of making some very good girlfriends in the biz who have helped me keep my head on straight about the whole issue. Although I'm still very aware of my diet, I have a much healthier perspective these days.

Here's the bottom line: If I really need to starve myself to be an actress in Hollywood, I'll find another line of work. I could always go behind the cameras as a director (that's a long-range goal of mine), or maybe as a producer. Or I could go back to college and pursue a completely different career. Of course, acting is still my first love. I'm so happy in front of the cameras. But let's be clear about this: I'm not going to make myself miserable and send myself into an emotional tailspin trying to rise to some impossible ideal! As much as I love acting, I could do something else.

With each passing day, I think I'm strengthening the healthy attitude I now have about food, diets, and the person I see in the mirror. But it hasn't happened overnight. It's taken a long, long time to get to this point. Because of the industry I work in, it's always going to be important for me to be conscious of what I weigh; Hollywood is absolutely obsessed with how people look, and as long as I'm a working actress, I can never lose sight of that. But fortunately, many of my close friends—inside and outside of show business—have a levelheaded point of view about diets and weight. Although we hear the message that "you can't be too thin"—the truth is, you definitely can! Everyone knows that eating disorders can be hazardous to your health: damaging vital organs, impairing the thyroid gland, and even causing cardiac arrest and death. Thousands of people, most of them young women, die each year as a direct result of anorexia or bulimia. Why would someone risk her life just to impress a casting director or producer? It's absolutely insane!

Even so, I know so many actresses who have suspended good judgment and continue to be caught up in self-starvation. They only seem to have their sights focused on the short-term goal, which is staying thin and getting and keeping their acting jobs. I see it all the time.

But I won't let this way of life grab ahold of me like it once did. I can't allow it to take me over and affect how I feel about myself. I really have learned to accept and love myself, whether I'm ten pounds heavier or ten pounds lighter than I was a month or two earlier. Yes, I know I'm never going to be pencil-thin—but I do want to be as healthy as possible. So I try to eat right because it's a way to stay healthy, not because I'm driven to fit the mold of the actress-with-the-perfect-body. Once I shifted my focus away from the scale and more toward leading a fulfilling, healthy life, my excess weight started to disappear.

It took me years to change my thinking to get to this place, and I have a much happier and wiser perspective about weight than I once did.

These days, I don't weigh myself. Ever. While I guess I have a general sense of what the number on the scale would be, it means much less to me than how my clothes look on me when I gaze into the mirror. If I look good in a favorite dress (I wear a size 2 or 4 today), that's all the motivation I need. I can see the payoff that comes with maintaining a healthy and comfortable weight. I'm also honest with myself—if the clothes are getting a little snug, it's time to back away from the cookie jar!

Sometimes, fans write me letters that say something like, "How can I get my daughter to lose weight like you did?" Well, just like I decided not to include a formal diet in this book, I decided not to give fans anything more than just some general information about what I did that finally worked for me. In the same way, you should find your own path. Someday, if I have a Ph.D. after my name or training as a registered dietitian, then maybe I'll get more specific. But for now, all I can really do is tell you about the success I've had, and suggest that everyone figure it out for herself. Find a way of eating that you can live with, and then stick with it. I hope you reach your weight-loss goals. But more than anything, I want you to be happy with yourself, no matter what your size. It really shouldn't matter what you weigh; if you don't look like the models on the cover of *Cosmo*, you can't spend your life feeling miserable about it.

Fans also sometimes ask for my thoughts about dietary supplements, which I've used on occasion (you may have seen me in TV commercials and print ads for a supplemental product not long ago). I've used supplements to maintain the weight loss I've already achieved, and to kick-start my workouts for bathing-suit scenes, and so forth. If you're like me, you've probably discovered that while losing weight is always a challenge, it's even more difficult to keep it off. And because of my unpredictable work schedule—where many hours can go by without time to eat, and where the buffet table near the set is always a temptation—I've sometimes used supplements as a safety net, helping me control my appetite, particularly when I have weak moments. Some supplements can speed up metabolism, making workouts more effective, and they can also make you thirsty, so you end up drinking lots of water (which is good for appetite control). But let me make this clear: I've *never* overused or overrelied on these supplements, and I refuse to let myself become dependent on them. I know that some people have had problems with certain supplements (although not the one I've helped promote) when they've overdone it, using them day after day (often several times a day), frequently at very high doses. When I've used supplements, it's only in moderation and with common sense as a guide. As with so many things, it's all about moderation.

As I tell my story in this book, I think I do have an important message to communicate—in particular to teenage girls and young women. As you mature and find where you fit into the world, don't let Hollywood dictate the way you need to look or how you feel about yourself if you don't have the "perfect body." You don't need to be a size 0 to pursue your dreams. The world isn't going to come to an end if you don't fit the stereotype of whatever happens to be the "right look" at the moment. Just be yourself, and your friends and family will love and appreciate you for it.

Chapter 14

Are you a couch potato?

Sound appealing?

There are times when the thought of living a sedentary lifestyle seems pretty attractive. Imagine curling up on the sofa in front of the fireplace and getting lost in a good novel all afternoon, barely moving hour after hour—and there's a time and a place for that! But it's the exception, not the rule.

I know better than to get too comfortable being lazy. Not only for my physical health, but also for my psychological well-being, I need to keep active.

Since some of this book has discussed weight and dieting, I can't neglect the importance of incorporating physical activity into an overall weight loss and fitness program. But as with my approach to dieting in this book, I'm not going to recommend a specific exercise plan that *you* should be following. That's not my purpose here. However, I will spend a few pages telling you what *I* do—what works for me . . . what keeps me in shape . . . what helps maintain my weight at a comfortable level. The foods I put on my plate, of course, are very important to keeping my weight where I want it. But exercise is just as essential to my lifestyle. It burns calories. It makes me feel better. It gives me more energy to keep pace with my hectic schedule.

It's like that billboard I've seen at malls lately. It says in big letters, "The Miracle Diet Pill," with a picture of a pill below it. But in black letters, one side of the pill says "diet" and the other side says "exercise." That really is the only way to get and stay fit—eating right, and exercise, exercise, exercise!

The Value of Exercise

For as long as I can remember, I've known the importance of exercise. For starters, as someone who once kept one eye on the scale, I can tell you that losing weight is much more difficult unless you're staying active and burning calories. Trust me, that's a no-brainer. However, bear in mind that when you exercise, you just might find yourself also gaining muscle mass, which will slow the speed of your weight loss. That's often what has happened with me when I work out. Yes, exercise keeps me healthy and fit, and it does help produce the loss of unwanted pounds over time. But it may not translate into an immediate lightning strike of weight loss when you expect it to.

Nevertheless, don't underestimate the ability of your workouts to contribute to your overall weight management. In fact, just spend a little time traveling through

Europe, and you'll see firsthand the value of physical activity. The United States has many more overweight people than France and most other European countries do, and you can't blame all of it on genetics. Yes, I'm sure there are some dietary factors at play: The French are much less reliant than Americans on high-fat fast food, and when they do eat rich cheeses, they keep the portions small—just enough to fit on a cracker or two! They eat slower, and they eat less. But perhaps most important, *they walk constantly.* The French aren't as reliant on automobiles as we are, and they wear out a lot more shoes than tires. Yes, New Yorkers walk a lot, but in most other American cities, people are hooked on their cars. No wonder obesity isn't as big a problem in Europe as it is here.

Making Fitness a Priority

Although I've always known that exercise is good for me, it was really driven home by Dr. Jay, my dentist, who I wrote about in Chapter 12. (Remember, he was the one who described me as "puffy," which I guess was better than calling me "fat"—but not by much!) I followed Dr. Jay's way of eating as closely as I could, but mostly he convinced me to reevaluate the way I was leading my life. And for Dr. Jay, exercise has been just as important as eating right. "You need to work out to be healthy," he told me.

Of course, I knew Dr. Jay was right, and for most of my life, I have been physically active. All I had to do was think back to my childhood, when, like most kids, I never stopped moving. Most children are outside playing from morning 'til night, and they're burning calories all the while. When you're that age and that active, having a Haagen-Dazs ice cream cone during the day is really not going to matter. But once life became much busier in adolescence and adulthood, I found that I needed to make fitness a priority or I'd never find time for it.

These days, I have to schedule my workouts just as I do every other appointment in the day. It needs to be as important as any other event or meeting. Listen, I block out time for doctor's appointments or meetings with my agent, right? So why not do the same for my workout? And on those days when I'm just not in the mood for physical activity, it's harder to feel lazy when I've already blocked out the 4 o'clock hour to get moving!

Now, let's put things in perspective: I've never been a person who wakes up in the morning and says, "I can hardly wait to get on the treadmill today!" For so many years, I just wasn't dedicated to my workouts. For a while, it became a real chore for me to get myself out the door to walk through the neighborhood or head for the gym. I'd force myself to do it at least two or three times a week, but my motivation sometimes waned if I didn't see much change in my weight (which was often the case because I was building up muscle mass). When that happened, I'd often throw in the towel for a month or two. I'd just take off my sneakers and store them in the closet for a while.

But since my heart-to-heart talk with Dr. Jay, physical fitness has become a way of life. For me, my workouts not only helped me lose weight, but even more important, they sure have helped *maintain* my current weight. They also make a huge difference in the way I feel.

How often do I exercise now? I don't feel the need to make it a six- or seven-day-a-week habit. But if I'm not lacing up my gym shoes three or four times a week, I've definitely fallen short of my goal. In fact, I've gotten to the point where I often actually crave those workouts—not only enjoying the activity itself, but also the adrenaline rush afterward. You've probably heard about the "runner's high"—that sense of exhilaration that can last long after you've wiped away the perspiration and showered. Exercise releases brain chemicals called *endorphins* that are known to produce a feeling of well-being. When you challenge your body—even if you're tired after the workout—the positive aftereffects are truly amazing!

I also don't overdo it when I work out (what would be the point of that?). I certainly don't have to push myself to the brink of exhaustion to get something out of it, nor does my workout have to be complicated. When I get my adrenaline flowing and my muscles working to the max (or close to it), that's all it takes—and this comes from someone who often hated exercising in the past! Recently, I saw a news story about a study involving two workout groups; it found that the women who worked out for less time but more intensely didn't lose any more weight than women who did a lower stress workout for a longer period of time. So walking uphill on the treadmill for forty-five minutes is right up my alley (so to speak).

Some people describe themselves as being "addicted" to exercise (how cool is that!). I might not go that far, but my workouts are the best means I've found for relieving the stresses and anxieties of the day. No matter what mood I've been in before my workout, I *always* feel better after a spirited game of basketball or a brisk walk in the park. I've also found that exercise tends to dampen my appetite and strengthen my resolve to stick with my eating plan (let's get real—after exercising for thirty minutes, you may not want to spoil the benefits you've achieved by splurging on a dessert that isn't part of the diet you're following). Exercise also elevates your calorie-burning metabolism not only during your workout, but also in the minutes and hours afterward. And as I've already mentioned, a good workout should give you much more energy during the day than if you had chosen to skip your exercise session.

How Much? How Often?

Over the years, I've tried tons of workout programs, sometimes even using a personal trainer who has helped me create an exercise plan and learn to use the equipment at the gym. And here's what I've found: What works best for me is to vary my exercise routines from one session to the next, with no rigid routines that have to be followed—or else!

Maybe I'll walk on the treadmill one day, use my stationery bike during the next workout, and walk my dog the following one (Dave and I have three dogs—Paco, Consuela, and Frieda). Then I might take a cardio-workout class at the gym on the fourth exercise day of the week. Sports can be fun, so I may play volleyball on the beach with friends, or test my skills in a touch football or basketball game for a change of pace (hmm, still no pro contracts being offered!). Dave and I also play racquetball as often as twice a week for two hours at a time (yes, this can really be exhausting!). I love skiing, too—in fact, my favorite travel destinations can be narrowed down to anyplace with a ski slope!

I also spent two years learning to kickbox (how 'bout

that!). I started kickboxing when Patrick Muldoon told me about a kickboxing gym that he had been going to in Santa Monica. I figured it was something I had to try, and I stuck with it for a couple years and got a lot out of it. But eventually, it became impractical to keep it up; the commute to the gym just got to be too taxing, and I looked for ways to exercise closer to home. Before long, I started going to a boxing gym just ten minutes from home. Austin Peck told me about it, and I took one-on-one classes there. I actually put on the gloves and sparred in the ring with a trainer! Can't you just picture me?! I wasn't quite ferocious enough to strike fear into the hearts of Muhammad Ali and George Foreman, but it sure was great fun and wonderful exercise.

By varying my workouts as much as possible, it keeps them from becoming repetitive and routine. And whether I'm in the mood to be alone or with other people, to be indoors or outdoors, there's always a form of exercise I can do.

I'm certainly not a jock, but I realize that I don't have to be. I love to take long walks, and let me tell you, almost *everybody* can walk (even you, even me!). It doesn't matter how young or how old you are, whether you're overweight and out of shape or have the finely tuned body of an Olympic athlete. You don't need expensive clothing or costly shoes to walk, either, nor do you need to join a gym. An hour-long brisk walk (moving at about three to four miles per hour) burns 300 to 400 calories, which can really add up, day after day. And here's what you'll find: Once you've been walking for a while, it gets easier. You'll be able to walk farther as you get in better shape.

Well, now that I've given you an idea of my favorite types

of workouts, here's some additional food for thought: Formal exercise isn't always necessary. *Any* kind of movement helps; even cleaning the kitchen (ugh!) or gardening burns calories and adds to your overall fitness, a little at a time. But that's not all. Stairs are everywhere, and if you walk up a flight or two instead of taking the elevator, it all counts. Park farther away from the mall entrance next time! It all contributes to your overall fitness. In my own case, I love gardening, and the calories it burns do accumulate. Swing dancing is another one of my passions, and it's a fabulous form of exercise.

(Author's personal collection)

Taking a ride with Ghost

When I'm ranking my preferences for physical activity, I've told you about nearly all of them, with one exception: Let's not forget the ponies! I've been horseback riding since I was a little girl, and when you're really working with your horse, whether it's a mare or a stallion, it's a great form of exercise and an awesome experience! When I was a kid, I took horseback-riding lessons almost every other day (I was so allergic to horses that I had to take allergy medicine just to get through the lessons—but that's how much I loved horses!). Today, I'm lucky to have my own horse, Apparition (with the nickname Ghost!).

For all the years of great experiences riding and competing, I will never forget the most embarrassing moments. One time, on a very (and I do mean *very*) hot day in Los Angeles, I was at a local horse show. I was wearing the usual competitive riding attire—long britches, long-sleeved shirt, wool coat—they weren't exactly perfect duds for a 100-degree afternoon. To make the situation worse, I wasn't drinking as much water as I should have. Well, you can guess what happened: In the middle of the course, all by myself in the ring and with all eyes on me, I began feeling weak, dizzy, and then very faint. Before I knew it, I had toppled off my horse and hit the ground with an ungraceful thud. Ouch! What I remember most about the incident was my mom and my trainer Nancy bringing me Gatorade and then helping me back onto the horse. The saying is completely true—you have to "get back on the horse" right away; otherwise you never will. I got onto his back again, jumped the jump, and learned a good lesson about myself. I may be afraid—but I won't let it stop me! Afterwards, I took off my coat and poured water on my head. Then I felt OK. But I was SO embarrassed!

Getting Motivated

OK, we all agree that exercise is important, whether we're doing it to lose weight or just to stay healthy. But as I mentioned at the beginning of this chapter, sometimes the couch looks awfully inviting. Motivating myself to get moving is still occasionally a challenge, and judging from some of the letters I get, many of my fans have the same problem—how to get inspired to put on the walking shoes and get going. One letter writer described it this way:

Dear Alison—I was an active child and teenager involved in many sports, and many of the same activities you enjoy. But as an adult, I've always had trouble finding the motivation to start a diet and exercise program because the results aren't always noticeable right away. Once I start to see some positive results, I can get motivated and get going, and I don't always need that extra outside push when it comes to exercising.

How did you get in such good cardiovascular shape, and did you do any strength training along with your workout? And who did you turn to for support when you found yourself having a tough day or not wanting to exercise (other than your husband)? Was getting started ever a problem for you? How did you get yourself motivated in the beginning and stay motivated throughout? I would greatly appreciate any feedback or advice you might have for me. I look forward to watching your continuing quest for optimum health.

Sincerely, Kimberly

There are times when in only an instant, I can weave out of thin air an excuse for not exercising! Maybe I didn't sleep well the night before, and I'm so tired. Or perhaps it's too hot outside (or too cold or too rainy). Or maybe I have to get up early the next morning to catch a flight. But when your choice of an exercise is convenient and just seconds away, it makes it harder to procrastinate, and much tougher to delay or dawdle. Unless I'm truly sick or injured, it's so much easier to stick with a workout program when it's readily available.

One of the best aspects of walking is that it's so convenient. It's harder to make excuses to stay on the couch when walking is on the agenda. Yes, there are days when I just don't feel like getting into the car and driving to the gym; it turns exercise into a bigger production than I'm prepared for. But to get ready for a walk through my neighborhood, all I need to do is put on my walking shoes and step out the door. Could it get any easier?

Sure, I still have days when I'd just rather not exercise. But here's something that I've found: I love to read, and I'll often get caught up in a book for hours. So rather than just reading while sitting in a comfortable chair, I'll slip on a pair of sweats and climb onto the exercise bicycle with my book, usually for thirty minutes at a stretch. I can read just as well when my feet are pedaling, and before I know it, I've finished twenty-five or fifty pages and have barely been aware that I've worked out (except for the beads of perspiration that have dripped onto the book!). The time goes by so fast!

Here's an additional component of this entire issue of motivation, and it has to do with your partner (Husband? Wife? Friend? You fill in the blank). While I know that my workouts help me maintain my weight where I want it, my husband Dave has *never* had a problem with weight. He has a very high metabolism that always seems to be in fourth gear. He can eat anything he wants and exercise as much or as little as he has time for, and he's not going to gain a pound. (As I've told him, "If we could bottle what's inside your body, we'd be multibillionaires!") If I let it, it would drive me crazy knowing how easily Dave maintains his weight and how I always need to stay vigilant. But I've got to admit, Dave *does* work hard at staying healthy, and he motivates me to keep going. We exercise together whenever possible. Sometimes we'll take long walks on the beach or just through the neighborhood. It's a great way for us to spend time together.

If you enjoy walking like us, change your route every day—it's a great way to become reacquainted with sections of your neighborhood that you might not have seen for a while, and you'll enjoy the change in scenery. (By the way, I know where Dave's enthusiasm for exercise comes from: His parents walk almost every day, keeping a steady pace both up and down the hills near their home. They're very inspirational!)

Staying Fit! Staying Slim!

There are plenty of other calorie-burning and fitness strategies that take almost no time, but go a long way toward keeping you fit. Here are just a few that are easy to fit into the day's activities, some of which I've already mentioned:

- When you're shopping—whether at the supermarket or the mall—park your car at the far end of the park-

ing lot and walk the equivalent of a block or two to
get to the store entrance.

- When you're visiting an office building, use the stairs
  rather than the elevator (if you need to go up more
  than just a couple floors, get off the elevator two or
  three floors before your stop and take the stairs the
  rest of the way).

- Take advantage of every opportunity to walk—for example, when you need to pick up some milk at the
  convenience store, walk instead of drive. You can also
  walk while you talk, using a cordless phone or a cell
  phone when calling friends. Two of my coworkers,
  Bryan Dattilo (Lucas) and Peter Reckell (Bo), often
  bicycle into work from their homes. Talk about getting your cardio in! It keeps them both incredibly fit!

- When you're looking for something to do on a weekend afternoon, take a family hike through the nearby
  mountains instead of taking in a movie.

You get the point, right? With a little creative thinking,
you can work exercise into your days without any real
strain.

Defining Health and Fitness

Before I close this chapter, let me make another very important point. I probably define health and fitness a little
broader than many other people. Health and fitness mean
more than just exercising regularly and keeping my body
in shape and well-toned, as important as that is. It means
more than working out or choosing my diet carefully. To

feel truly healthy, both physically and psychologically, I'm committed to being as happy and content as possible in every aspect of my life. That means pursuing a career that brings me fulfillment. It means caring about others and making time for friends, even if it's just a group of us hanging out and talking late into the night. It means minimizing the stress that I know can take a toll on my body—making sleep difficult, and over time leading to illness and depression.

It means being more accepting of myself, with all my strengths and all my weaknesses. It means setting goals and working hard to achieve them. It means being willing to change as my life evolves. It means trying to make every year better than the last one . . . and not beating myself up when I indulge once in a while! ☺

Chapter 15

(Author's personal collection)

We took this shot in front of the plane. Dave and I fly all over the place with our plane for mini-vacations. In fact, we often take our puppies with us.

I'm always fascinated by some of the questions that viewers of *Days of Our Lives* ask me in their fan mail—or, for that matter, what reporters ask in interviews for newspapers or the soap magazines. Of course, I understand the curiosity of fans about what goes on at *Days*; in fact, that's one of the reasons I wrote this book. For most *Days* fans, missing even a single episode would be unimaginable. For them, watching *Days* is a serious commitment—it's something they can't seem to live without. They never miss the show, and if they're at work or out-of-town on weekday afternoons, their VCR is preset and ready for action.

Judging by my mail, fans want to know just as much about me and the show's other actors as about the heartaches and happiness that our characters are experiencing. Where did we meet our real-life spouse (or boyfriend), and if we're single, who are we dating? Who are our friends, both on and off the set? Where do we like to shop? What

(Author's personal collection)

Riding a moped around Tahiti with Dave on our honeymoon

lipstick was I wearing in that scene on Tuesday in Salem Place? What do we do for fun? What advice do we have for their own romantic problems?

Because we're invited into America's living rooms five days a week, many fans feel that we're part of their family, and that they know almost everything about us, or at least want to. They're never hesitant to ask questions or offer advice. It's really quite a unique relationship.

In this chapter and the next one, let me describe all you've ever wanted to know about Alison Sweeney that I haven't written about thus far—well, maybe not *all!* And don't worry—if there are questions I haven't answered in this book, I'll keep reading and answering your fan mail. And if these pages spark any new questions, drop me a line and I'll do my best to fill in the blanks.

My Home Life

I'm amazed at how much fans know about my life with my husband, Dave. While I'm used to having the spotlight shine on me, Dave's the kind of guy who is quite content staying out of the public eye, and as I've mentioned, he works in a profession (law enforcement) that has nothing to do with show business. So while he's not particularly eager for attention, he's married to me and so he knows that some of it comes with the territory. We can't go out in a public place and expect that we'll always be able to enjoy a quiet dinner without a fan approaching from another table and asking for an autograph or a photo. Neither of us minds it—a *Days* viewer may appear and just want to spend a few moments with us. For the most part, however, Dave and I lead a very normal, very private life. (Let's face it, after acting in a soap opera all day, where the story lines and our characters' behavior can border on the unusual—including the predictable hell-raising of Sami—I need the calmness and stability that Dave brings to my life.)

When did I meet Dave? Well, we've known each other for as long as either of us can remember—literally! My mother and Dave's father worked together for many years; both of them are violinists whose talents you've probably heard on many motion picture soundtracks. Our families have always been friendly, and so I knew Dave when we were growing up. In fact, when I was about ten years old, I had quite a crush on him, although I'm sure he didn't know it; he was older (about fourteen years old at the time) and, of course, he couldn't be bothered with a kid

(Lesley Bohm)

Unlike Sami, I've been
very lucky in love.

like me when he was meeting girls his own age. Before
long, Dave went to college; we lost contact for a while, but
we saw each other again at a party at his parents' house in
1997—he was twenty-four at the time, and I was about to
turn twenty-one. There was definitely a lot of chemistry

there—and if you're wondering, there still is!!!—and I just couldn't take my eyes off of him. Before that night ended, I invited him to my twenty-first birthday party. One thing led to another ... and here we are, living happily ever after!

Once we were a couple, things happened very quickly. We have so much in common, and there was never a question in my mind that he was Mr. Right (I know that sounds pretty cheesy, but it's absolutely true!).

After dating for several months, Dave gave me a big-time clue of what the future might hold. "Someday," he said, "I'm going to ask you to marry me, and we're going to spend the rest of our lives together." Wow! That was so amazing! That's not something that you'd expect to hear from most guys. But early on, he was already thinking about making a commitment. Well, guess what: I was already feeling the same way!

I'll never forget my first Valentine's Day with Dave. It was sooo romantic! Now, Dave doesn't particularly enjoy musical theater, but it's never been a secret that I absolutely love it! (Hey, remember our *Moulin Rouge* productions at Fan Weekends?!). So (leave it to Dave!) he planned a Valentine's evening for us at the theater, which meant so much to me (I knew it wouldn't have been *his* first choice of an ideal night on the town). We also had a *very* romantic dinner in downtown L.A., not far from the theater in an incredible high-rise restaurant with a spectacular view of the entire city. It was an absolutely wonderful evening (Dave, I still remember that Valentine's Day—it was so special!).

By the way, now that Dave and I are married, Valentine's Day may be even more important to us. Once you're married, it's less about trying to impress the other person and more about taking the time to have some special moments together; it's a wonderful occasion for spoiling your significant other, setting aside some time for romance and cuddling, and keeping the fires burning (if you get my drift!). Because our respective schedules can be so hectic, we often end up celebrating Valentine's Day sometime in the vicinity of February 14th when both of us have free time, but often missing the exact day. Both of us also have a knack for finding humorous, sweet cards for one another, and we usually exchange small personal gifts. But the most important part is that we've set aside a night to be together.

Well, I've already given you examples of how romantic Dave can be. But I haven't described the night he proposed marriage. That's a night I'll *never* forget! We went to Catalina Island—26 miles off the coast of Los Angeles—for a quick getaway. Nothing seemed particularly out of the ordinary—Dave appeared easygoing and low-key when the weekend began. But then it all changed. At his suggestion, we took a stroll along the boardwalk by the ocean and exchanged small talk for a few minutes. But once we reached a secluded spot on the sand, the mood changed (did it ever!). I looked over and Dave had knelt down on one knee. Oh my God, I almost died! Before I could catch my breath or say a word, he proposed to me on the spot. I was *so* shocked—and so happy! Fortunately, my part in this monumental and memorable event was pretty small: All I really had to say was "yes"—Dave took care of everything else! Now, *that* was definitely one of the most romantic moments of my life!

Although Dave and I didn't get married right away, it

(Author's personal collection)

One of Sami's many wedding styles . . . she should write a book!

seemed like the planning was upon us before long—and let me tell you, making all the arrangements can be very involved and time-consuming! I knew that this was the one and only time I'd ever get married, and I wanted everything to be just right. But I didn't realize that there are so many things to organize, to plan for and keep track of, and it's so easy to overlook some of the tiny details if you're not careful.

At first, I wanted Dave to help me plan everything—but that didn't last long! Yes, we both picked out the location, agreeing on an outdoor wedding near the ocean; we reached those kinds of really big decisions together. But he finally admitted to me that he would prefer to let me do all the "girly" stuff that he didn't have much interest in, which was just fine. I continued to ask his opinion on a lot of things—but I called a lot of the shots myself (with the help of my mom!), and I just hoped Dave would agree with them (which he usually did). Even when my mom and I differed on some of the details, we'd sit back and say, "Let's think about what each of us has in mind, and we'll come back and work it out so everyone's happy!" And we always did!

Everybody had told me in advance that when I went shopping for my wedding dress, I'd know it when I saw it (although I had my doubts about that). On *Days of Our Lives*, I had already worn three wedding gowns on the show, and so I wasn't sure that I was going to have this magical feeling when I finally chose the one for my own wedding. I spent a lot of time visiting different shops and trying on plenty of styles. I listened to everyone's opinions. Luckily, my best friend Carrie was there with me—and more than looking at each dress, she'd look at my face, and she could tell right away if the dress was "the one" or not. Once I had found the dress that I eventually chose, guess what? The first time I tried it on, I knew immediately that this was the one . . . this was the perfect dress for me. I was certain it was right, and I never had any second thoughts.

Dave and I were married in July 2000, and before the big day, *Entertainment Tonight*'s producers contacted me about sending a camera crew to tape the event for airing on their show. Well, as I've mentioned, Dave doesn't seek

(Robert Sebree)

the limelight, but he said OK about the TV coverage, although he did add, "Just don't make me talk a lot!" I know he liked the idea of having professional cameramen cover the wedding from beginning to end (we were promised a copy!), and they sure did a great job—there were shots of me getting ready (with the curling iron working overtime!), images of me walking down the aisle with my father, the vows themselves, the exchange of rings, and the reception afterward, including our first dance. And, of course, there were glimpses of the cast of *Days* congratulating us, and partying into the night.

(Robert Sebree)

Dave's dad and my mom performed a duet during our wedding ceremony. Here we are applauding their beautiful performance.

Of the *Days* cast, Bryan Dattilo, Arianne Zucker, Jensen Ackles, Matt Cedeno, and Josh Taylor were able to attend. I have such a great photo of all us toasting with champagne. And my dad was so cute—he mentioned my "*Days* Dad" in his Father-of-the-Bride speech. What a day, and thanks to *Entertainment Tonight*, we have a great wedding video, and of course, some wonderful memories. It also meant a lot to me that my fans got to share in our special day when it aired on *ET*!

If you're a young woman thinking about or actually planning your wedding, here's my advice: Never lose sight of the fact that this will be one of the most memorable days of your life. So don't let yourself stress out too much over it. On *Days of Our Lives*, I've taken part in many on-screen weddings that were wrecked by one unbelievable disaster or another—but I just knew that my own wedding was going to be great, and that any minor glitches sure weren't going to spoil the party. Nothing was more important than enjoying the day. And we sure did!

A few months after Dave and I were married, two of my best friends on *Days*—Ari Zuker and Julianne Morris—and I joked with Ken Corday (our executive producer) at a Christmas lunch that we were all going to walk into his office on the same day and announce that all of us were pregnant! Now, wouldn't that have turned his life upside down?!

Friendships and Relationships

When you think of Sami Brady, it's hard to imagine anyone who is more adept at ruining relationships, including her own (OK, maybe there are a few other characters on *Days* who could give her a run for her money from time to time!). Nevertheless, despite Sami's sinister side, fans still often write to me for advice, figuring that I probably bring more sanity and common sense to these issues than Sami might.

One subject they ask a lot about is friendships, although I'm not sure I'm a real authority on the topic. When I joined the cast of *Days*, I was in my teens, and even though everyone was very nice to me, I saw my fellow actors as "work friends"—not to be confused with "personal friends." I frequently kept to myself on the studio lot, often doing homework in my dressing room. But I eventually realized that these cast members were very special people, and I became much more comfortable around them. I started hanging out with people like Julianne and Ari, and today, some of the *Days* cast members are among my best friends. Those friendships were there right in front of me the entire time; I just didn't realize it. Overall, I learned it is more important to have a handful of great friendships than a plethora of mediocre ones. I work to make time for my girlfriends and my husband, and they are all rewarding and meaningful relationships.

But while friendships are a common theme in my fan mail, there's a much more pressing issue that girls and young women often ask about—how can they get guys interested in them? Or how can they keep boys from hurting them? Or how far should they go? Or what's the best way to break up or make up with boyfriends? These letters come mostly from teenage girls who somehow think that I hold all the keys to successful dating. (Little do they know. . . .)

When those letters arrive, however, I do answer them,

and sometimes give some general advice. (I'm no Dr. Laura, but I do have an opinion about almost everything!) Thinking back to high school, those teenage years can be such a challenge—just trying to make good friends, much less having and keeping a boyfriend. In my own case, I was terribly shy and insecure, consumed with the belief that I was overweight and very average looking. When it came to school dances and parties, I certainly wasn't part of the popular crowd, and to me, my life seemed pretty uneventful and uninteresting compared to theirs. I wanted to have more friends than I did.

So I struggled with friendships for such a long time. Having a boyfriend almost seemed out of the realm of possibility—at least that's the way I viewed it. Looking back, I wish I had been a little more assertive with boys. I sometimes tell teenage girls not to be afraid to make the first phone call or the first move with boys. I had such a lack of confidence during adolescence that it never crossed my mind that boys might actually like me. Only years later did I realize that, yes, maybe some of those cute boys in school did give me a second glance from time to time.

Dear Ali—I know you'll be married soon so you have experience with relationships. People say I'm pretty nice, but my problem is that guys always hurt me. I've been crushing on a guy from work for a long time. He knows how much I care for him because we're friends. And we dated a lot last summer. But then he started pulling away. Tonight someone made an innocent comment about him having a girlfriend. I felt like I had been punched. So my questions are, "How do you get guys to stay interested in you? How do you know when someone really cares about you or if they're just using you?" This person is someone who knows so much about me. And I always believed he cared. He's not just a "talker." Still, why couldn't he tell me the truth?

I know you probably don't get many letters like this one. So I'm sorry. I shouldn't dump my problems on you. I just look up to you and would appreciate any thoughts and advice.

Love, Kelly

When I answer mail like this, I may include comments from the vantage point of someone in her mid-twenties with at least some life experience. More than anything, I tell fans that no matter what their age or circumstances, be true to yourself when it comes to boys and men (and everything else in life, for that matter). I know that's sometimes so hard to do. But step one: I encourage girls to work on building their self-confidence and on liking the person they are.

Too often, of course, we don't make the best decisions when it comes to boys and men. One colleague of mine had a boyfriend who's an actor, and many of her waking hours were devoted to keeping him happy. She had suffered from anorexia in the past, and amid the stress of this relationship, found herself slipping back into eating behaviors that bordered on self-starvation. She tried desperately to compete with the models he dated when he wasn't going out with her. She wanted his attention so badly that she was literally willing to put her own health on the line. All for the "love" of a man.

Another friend had a boyfriend who didn't treat her

well at all. In fact, he beat her up, and did it more than once. (How disgusting is that?!) But here's the ironic part: Not only is she beautiful, outgoing, and funny, she is also one of the strongest and most assertive young women I've ever met—except when relating to her boyfriend. She finally found the strength to untangle herself from that relationship, but when she told me and the rest of our friends about the abuse she had taken, we were so upset that we were ready to kick his ass ourselves! She did eventually learn to stand up for herself, and she has created very healthy relationships for herself since then. (It's like that Christina Aguilera song, "Thanks for making me a fighter!")

I've also known young women who have gone through one imperfect relationship after another and have become so desperate for marriage that they're willing to settle for something less than what they really want. One of my girlfriends comes immediately to mind. All she wants is to meet the right guy, get married, and raise a family with him. At one point, she tried to convince the rest of us that the man she was dating at the time was perfect for her. Yes, he was very good-looking. Yes, he was definitely in love with her. But there was a "minor" problem: She wasn't in love with him. Even though she really tried to *make* herself love him, it just didn't work. Yet she still drove herself (and at times the rest of us) crazy trying to convince everyone that she could somehow make their relationship work. That's how much she wanted a family, the house in the suburbs and the picket fence.

The dating world really is a jungle at times, isn't it? Maybe I'm lucky that before Dave and I began dating, I really didn't go out that much. I guess you could say that the dating scene wasn't my thing—okay, to be more accurate,

I was really picky!! I didn't go out just to be going out. I just didn't enjoy spending a lot of time with someone I wasn't sure I wanted to be with. Yes, there was a group of friends of both sexes who I hung out with a lot—we'd socialize as a group, play volleyball at the beach, or organize a tag football game. I went on individual dates from time to time, but looking back, I was *ultra*selective and not willing to put up with the craziness of dating if it wasn't for real. (No regrets!) In fact, Dave was the first and only man I ever had a serious, long-term relationship with—and I knew right away that he was the person I wanted to spend the rest of my life with!

(Author's personal collection)

Future prom king and queen?

For most of my life, my best friends have been actors, but I always had trouble seeing myself dating one. But here's a bit of trivia: If you want to go all the way back to high school, Bryan Dattilo was my date for the prom, and it may have been particularly memorable because a waiter recognized us from our work on *Days!* It was the first "fan experience" for both me and Bryan, and when you're not used to getting that kind of attention, it makes an impression!

A Word About Sex

Well, I know what you're thinking. With all this talk about men, boys, dating, and marriage, what about sex? As with most of these interpersonal issues, I'm not an expert, although you'd think I was, judging by the number of letters I get on the subject.

Here's what I do know: Many young girls are dressing more provocatively these days and seem to be having sex earlier than ever. While sex can be a wonderful and deeply fulfilling experience, it's also something that can undermine your self-esteem if it's not with the right person at the right time. As I sometimes tell teenagers, no matter what your friends are doing, and no matter how much pressure you're feeling, you should always feel free to say no. It's okay to wait if that's what you really want to do. There may be a lot of reasons to have sex, but if you decide to become intimate because you think it will help you keep your boyfriend or because it will help you fit in with one clique or another, that usually doesn't work.

When I was in high school, our teacher in human sex-

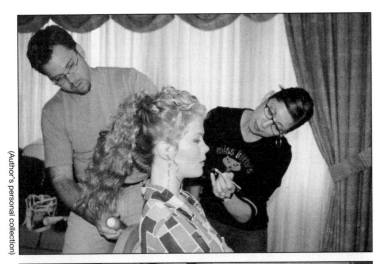

(Author's personal collection)

(Author's personal collection)

Having the right make-up artist and hairdresser are key—I am
very lucky to be friends with such talented artists!

uality class quoted a study that described the ultimate fantasy that girls have for their first time. Here's what it involved: The love of their life, romantic candles, and a bearskin rug. (Sound familiar?) But according to the study, 90 percent of the girls surveyed never get close to that dream. So I tell girls not to be held hostage by their (or his) hormones, and to use good judgment. Be true to yourself, and don't put yourself in situations that are difficult to get out of. (One recent study found that one in ten girls reported being raped or physically abused on dates.)

The bottom line: Sex is wonderful but it's also pretty serious business (no kidding!). Move at your own pace. Go slowly if that's what feels comfortable. Your time will come. And remember, it's your body. It's your life.

Fashion Statements

As an actress, I have to do photo shoots from time to time, and they can be a fun part of the job. It's a great chance to play dress-up, wearing a lot of different clothes that are provided for you. The costume designers and wardrobe stylists usually bring in a ton of dresses and outfits to choose from—although the stylists I work with on *Days* know pretty well the kinds of clothes I like, and those that I wouldn't wear in a million years.

I've always found these photo shoots to be so liberating. Once I'm in front of the photographer, and he's snapping one roll of 35mm film after another in rapid-fire fashion, it's a time when I can be absolutely uninhibited. I can strike sexy poses. I can make faces. I can act absolutely crazy. What a blast!

At the same time, however, photo shoots can be hard work. You're frequently striking poses and positions that are incredibly uncomfortable and awkward. ("Straighten your arm, okay, balance on your right elbow, now suck in that tummy, arch your neck . . . now look relaxed!!!") I once did a photo shoot in the Pacific Ocean, wearing a mermaid costume; it might have been L.A., but the water temperature was in the mid-50s, and I was so cold and miserable that I'd whimper in between each click of the camera.

On *Days*, we can choose the clothes we wear, but both the wardrobe department and the actors do have to pay very close attention, and here's why. When there's an on-going story line, I may have to wear the same dress every day for three weeks if that's what the script and the scenes call for; if the story lines are being shot out of order, it can get pretty complicated. There's also the small matter of trying to match the same hair style from one day's shooting to the next to maintain story continuity. God bless our makeup staff and hair stylists, who always seem to pull off the impossible.

As if you couldn't guess, I dress very differently than Sami in real life (it's another instance in which Sami and I are very different). When I'm trying on clothes for Sami—to see which ones I'm comfortable wearing and that fit well—I'm judging them as Sami, not as Ali. Clearly, Sami has her own style of dress that's much more revealing and sexier than my own. I'm much more often found in jeans or sweat pants, and Abercrombie & Fitch is one of my favorite clothing stores. But Sami's much more into fashion than I am.

At the same time, whether or not you're an actor, all of us want to look our best. Fashion fads come and go at supersonic speeds, and sometimes it seems that you can walk out of a mall with a shopping bag filled with new clothes, but by the time you get a chance to wear them, they could be painfully out of style. When I look back at the wardrobe I wore when I started on *Days*, I want to flinch and even laugh out loud. I wore a lot of preppy clothes—khaki pants, polo shirts, penny loafers. You get the picture. Even though the early 1990s weren't that long ago, now the fashions that were so popular then look like they belong in the Smithsonian Institution. Internet message boards are filled with critiques of every outfit that an actress wears, and most of them aren't particularly flattering.

What Are You Wearing?

As I've mentioned, in the stampede to be stylish, so many of today's teenage girls and young women are hooked on eye-catching, seductive, and sexually driven designer clothes. The fashion industry and the pop celebrities of the moment are selling themselves with provocative clothing that certainly gets them noticed—and for better or worse, they are often the trendsetters for girls who may be too young to dress in these same titillating styles. In this grow-up-fast culture, the fashion industry is marketing sex appeal, and many girls (some as young as ten years old and occasionally even younger) act like their world would end if they couldn't wear a Britney Spears look-alike outfit. But sometimes I ask myself, "What happened to their childhood?" I was wearing OshKosh B'Gosh clothing at age nine, and I certainly wasn't concerned about being trendy or sexy. But today, I swear that Lolita has nothing on some of these kids!

I tell adolescent girls and young women that it's silly to get sucked into a trend, particularly if it makes you cringe a little when you look in the mirror. We all have different body types, and what looks great on Christina Aguilera may be a bit embarrassing on most of us. Don't let Christina or Britney be the sole influence on how you should look in order to fit in. There are ways to be trendy without degrading yourself, and you don't have to reveal as much skin as some of today's superstars do.

Kids often don't realize that they're already beautiful and don't need to go overboard. As for the moms of these young girls, they sometimes tell me, "There's nothing I can do about it—she just wants to wear those Britney-type outfits!" Maybe a preteenager does want to dress that way, but moms can wield more influence than they think, especially since they're probably footing the bill for those overly revealing clothes!

From time to time, some girls actually write to complain that they just don't feel comfortable in the fashions of the day. I remind them that when it comes to fashion trends, the pendulum will swing the other way before long. Back when Madonna was the rage, my friends and I wore bangs (sprayed and teased to the max), rubber bracelets up to our elbows, and so much blue mascara that we actually looked a little scary. Now, I make sure that the old photos of me in that attire are buried deeply in my closet where no one can locate them. Not even me!

If you're a teenage girl, find a style that makes you look good and feel confident. Forget about what the current generation of Madonnas or other MTV icons are wearing at the moment, and choose clothes that are appropriate for your body type. It's so easy to get swept up by peer pressure and the clothing craze of the hour, but stick to the fashions that make you feel comfortable. Find clothes that show *you* off—not the clothes! You might even ask your mom to help choose your clothing, providing another set of eyes for what looks best on you. (How's that for sounding square!)

Let me make one other "fashion statement": I know there are certain kinds of clothes from head to toe that I look good in, and there are others that don't belong on or anywhere near my body! That even goes for shoes. Because I'm not particularly tall, I'm an ideal candidate to wear high heels. But I hate them! Sometimes I wish they didn't exist! Yes, I wear them when I have to, but that's not very often—I'm just not going to ruin my feet and my back just to fit the image of what someone else considers to be stylish.

My alternative: As I write these words, I'm wearing a particular pair of sneakers that have been my shoes-of-choice for months. Sneakers all winter, flip-flops all summer—that's my official dress code. You almost have to force me to try something different. But I've learned through hard-earned self-acceptance that even with those well-worn and tattered sneakers, I can still look pretty good, feel comfortable with myself, and spare my feet the unnecessary agony.

When push comes to shove, I'd choose to dress casually seven days a week if I could. I'm a jeans and T-shirt kind of gal, and if you spot me in a restaurant or at a mall, that's probably what I'll be wearing!

Chapter 16

Show business has been my life seemingly forever. But I wouldn't have it any other way. It's so fulfilling. It's so much fun. I truly believe that acting is what I was meant to do, and I'm so lucky to have had the opportunity to be part of the *Days of Our Lives* cast for so many years.

I remember telling a reporter not long ago that I find myself in something of a funny position. In some ways, I feel like a veteran on the show, and just in terms of the length of time I've been on *Days*, I am one of the "old guard." On the other hand, I'm still only 26 years old (as these words are written). At times, as younger and younger cast members have been added, I've thought, "I'm not the teenager, I'm not the new kid on the block anymore." It's been almost like going through a midlife crisis at the age of 26! Yet as each actor joins the show, I've often been able to help them learn the ropes when necessary, just the way

Deidre Hall and some of the others did when I started playing Sami. As I've already acknowledged, Deidre taught me so much, sometimes just by letting me watch her be the true professional she always is, but also by generously giving me instruction when I needed it about some of the basics—camera angles, lighting, hitting your marks, and saying your lines with confidence. I guess at some point, these younger actors will be there to help the next generation of *Days* stars.

Is Show Business in Your Future?

You've heard it before: When selecting a career, you couldn't choose one any tougher than show business. Yet as I mentioned in Chapter 3, parents often ask me whether this is a business that makes sense for their children, and young men and women ask whether they should chase their dreams of an acting career.

I know that I've been more fortunate than most actors—and I'm *so* grateful for the success that I've had. So many of my peers have had their dreams shattered and their spirits crushed by an industry that often seems to treat its talent like yesterday's newspaper. It's not fair, but that's the way it works. Of course, many people are drawn to Hollywood, attracted by the glamour, the celebrity, and the major paychecks they read about. But no matter how successful an actor has been, he or she is always aware that there are a hundred fresh new faces waiting in the wings, eagerly hoping to take the place of those already there. It can be a ruthless business, and even when careers get off the ground, they are often extinguished long before the actor is ready for it to end.

Jack Lemmon once described his career as "a one-in-a-million shot that worked." Sometimes, the odds seem as imposing as Lemmon suggested. Even so, there are a great many exciting and rewarding aspects to this life. I can't imagine being happier doing anything else. Even if I were still struggling to get my first acting jobs, I don't think I'd have any regrets. Actors have to act. I knew as a child that I wanted to tell stories on the stage or in front of the cameras. So I followed that passion, as so many others do— even when the jobs seem scarce and even when our spirits and morale are challenged.

Are you thinking of giving acting a shot? If you believe in yourself and believe in your talent, and if you feel you have what it takes to make it in this business, I encourage you to go for it. Whether you're seeking your first acting job or already have a growing list of credits, work at developing your craft at every opportunity. That's what I do. Even though I've been a working actress most of my life, there's still so much I want to learn. There are so many good acting teachers and college drama programs that there's no excuse for actors to be untrained. There's no justification for coming to the set or the stage unprepared. There is no reason to do your scenes on the fly, particularly if you want to have longevity in this career. Remember, this is a business, and you need to be ready when opportunities present themselves.

Sharpening Your Skills

Even though I'm able to refine my acting talents five days a week on *Days of Our Lives*, I still take acting lessons whenever I can squeeze them into my schedule. I've been doing that since I was a kid, when my brothers (Sten and Ryan) and I took just about every type of class or private lesson imaginable at one time or another. In my case, there were acting and commercial classes, not to mention piano, voice, ballet, tap, jazz, tennis, gymnastics, and trampoline lessons. I studied the violin for eight years and practiced hours every day. (That's a serious commitment!) I still have so much appreciation for classical music—I remember doing homework to Mozart during much of my child-hood—although I did eventually give up music lessons when there weren't enough hours in the day to do it justice.

I'm a firm believer that acting classes are not only a chance to practice and nurture your craft, but it's also valuable to have a skilled acting teacher or coach observing and guiding you. When you're like me—acting consistently, day after day—it would be very easy to get into bad habits. Nothing can take the place of someone with expertise watching what you do, offering constructive criticism, and guiding you on improving your performance. For me, one of the most exciting parts of acting is learning something new, developing my art, and gaining insights into the character I'm playing. And a good acting coach—one with an excellent track record—can analyze my performance, tell me what he or she sees, and help me take my acting to the next level so I'm not just "phoning it in," day after day.

I've always heard that "acting is reacting," and with that in mind, you need to develop the skill to *really listen* to what the other characters on the stage are saying, even though you're familiar with the script from top to bottom. Yes, you know their next line and you certainly know yours—but once the cameras are rolling, you have to make it look as though you've never heard it before. With the help of an acting coach, I've become much better at staying in the moment with my character, keeping her fresh, and avoiding the trap of unconsciously becoming lazy and overrelying on what I've done in the past. There's nothing worse than an actor who resorts to shortcuts or puts the performance on autopilot. If you're not careful, your character can become stale, and audiences sure notice.

My favorite classes are improvisational classes. Improv is such a fun technique—think *Whose Line Is It Anyway?* and you have an idea of how we spend a three-hour class. Whether you want to write, direct, or just become more comfortable speaking in public, improv is a great way to refine your skills and talents. I was even a member of the Los Angeles Theatresports Troupe for a few years, and I still keep in touch with them, still hoping to be able to perform from time to time. If you ever want to be highly entertained some night, go see an improv group—there are tons of sites that can guide you to local theaters. Enjoy!

To stay razor-sharp, I've enrolled in other classes—for example, one-on-one acting classes, group classes, and auditioning classes. I even still take dance classes now and then. OK, without a doubt, I know I'm *never* going to dance professionally, but I feel I can improve and get better at just about anything if I set my mind to it—and there are actually some acting benefits from my pursuit of dance. Let me tell you, I've made progress in every dance class, and as that has happened, I now have more control over my body and I'm more aware than ever of my posture, where my hands are, where I carry tension, and how my body movements project on camera. That has translated into improvement in my overall acting. There's always something to learn, and I'm always up for a challenge.

If you're an actor—whether you're just starting out or are already enjoying success—search for the learning environment that's best for you. It might be private coaching, or it could involve joining a group class. Whatever you choose, it can be an invaluable learning experience, and one that makes you a better actor. Do what it takes to move ahead—and stay optimistic.

If you don't already have an agent, you'll need one, so ask your actor friends for recommendations. A personal referral will help protect you from the Hollywood sharks—you know, the ones whose scams seem to be featured regularly on *20/20*. Be careful—con artists exist by the hundreds, preying on young people who are naïve about the business and don't really know what to expect and who to trust. About the only thing these pseudoagents are good at is taking your money and making it all sound reasonable. Be careful!

Once you start going on auditions, remember that your mission is to sell yourself. So be positive. Be enthusiastic. Become the actor they want to hire.

At the same time, acknowledge that some disappointments are almost inevitable. You might get rejected a dozen (or maybe a hundred) times for every acting job you get. Be prepared. Develop some thick skin. Become as resilient as possible if you're going to be in this business to stay.

If the Disappointments Mount . . .

I sometimes advise young actors that it's a good idea to have a fallback position. Listen, you should pursue your acting career with all the enthusiasm and positive energy you can muster, but sad to say, the bolt of lightning spelled F-A-M-E and S-U-C-C-E-S-S doesn't strike everyone. I encourage young people who want to be actors to go to college so they'll have the option to pursue another career if the acting life proves elusive. College is not only a great place to take acting classes, but it presents wonderful opportunities to meet other students and professors you can network with for the rest of your life. There's plenty to learn in college, and a lot of connections you can make during your four years on campus.

As I described in Chapter 4, I had planned to attend college and visited a number of campuses while I was in high school, trying to decide which university would be the best fit. But the opportunity to continue working on *Days of Our Lives* was just too good to pass up, and I decided to put my college dreams on hold. It was a very difficult decision—one of the hardest of my life—particularly because my family (especially my father) is so strongly committed to the value of an education. My dad was also concerned about how I would support myself if my acting career hit a tripwire or two. He felt that an education is something you can always fall back on (not to mention recognizing the importance of acquiring knowledge and challenging yourself each and every day). I love studying and reading about many topics, so someday I know I'll find the time to put in my four years at a university! Stay tuned . . .

My dad was certainly right about one thing—actually, he's been right about most things! (Thanks, Papa! ☺) He knew that the majority of actors don't have those Jack Lemmon-like careers that span a lifetime. When you think about it, so many actors have been on hit TV shows, but once the show has run its course, they're never heard from again. Success in one TV series or one motion picture doesn't guarantee that another acting job is right around the corner. Actresses in particular seem to be swimming upstream in a profession where youth is a huge asset. As I wrote in Chapter 10, there is a window of opportunity for most actresses, and if you don't catch the wave in your "prime" (before the Attack of the Gray Hair and Wrinkles!), your time as an actress might just pass you by. It's almost like being a competitive swimmer—age can be an enemy, and if you haven't won your share of ribbons by your midteens, the people who count may no longer take you seriously. (So unfair!)

A Little Diversification!

As I've suggested, I'm always up for a challenge! Sure, acting is my first love, but I also enjoy a little variety and have never been one to back away from a show-business dare. If someone tells me I can't do something—well, those are fightin' words! In fact, I've tried some things on television that I once couldn't have imagined myself doing. Here's an example or two: How about eating worms on national TV? Or balancing on a narrow ledge on the 36th floor of a Los Angeles office building?

Well, I can thank *Fear Factor* for providing some of my most death-defying moments on television. Unlike the execution chamber scene on *Days of Our Lives*, or the scenes where Sami was fighting for her life after being struck by a car driven by Austin, the *Fear Factor* segments were for real. They were *really* for real! One slip on that high-rise building, and the only thing between me and a close-up view of the street-level concrete would have been the strength of the safety harnesses.

How did my appearance on *Fear Factor* come about? I met the producer of the show at an NBC party, and I told him how much I loved the show and how grossed out I was watching a recent episode. He must have appreciated my attitude, and sure enough, he invited me to be on an upcoming celebrity episode of the show.

Actually, before *Fear Factor*, you may have seen me on a few game shows, most notably *The Weakest Link*. If you saw that program back in March 2002, you'll remember it as a Battle of the Soaps—some of us from *Days of Our Lives* competed with cast members from *Passions*—all of us playing for our favorite charities. And it was so much fun!! From *Days*, I was joined by Matt Cedeno (ex-Brandon), Jim Reynolds (ex-Abe), and Jason Cook (Shawn). And it really went down to the wire. I fought my way into the final round and ended up playing against Jim. And let me tell you, I got pretty concerned near the end. The championship was decided on my final question, which was: "What does the 'T' in 'ROTC' stand for?"

Oh, please! I had absolutely no idea!

I took a few seconds to collect my thoughts, and must have raced through a dozen or more words that started with "T". Still no clue. The only word that made any sense was "Training." So what the heck—I took a deep breath and gave it a try!

Amazing! It was the right answer! All of my friends and Dave back in the green room must have been working overtime sending mental-telepathy messages my way for me to get that one right!

James was so nice about it—he was genuinely happy for me. I was so excited to be able to send a big check to the charity I was playing for—the California Highway Patrol 11-99 Foundation. I won $68,500 for the foundation, and every penny went to these wonderful CHP widows and children who can certainly use the help.

Facing Down Fear

When I appeared on the celebrity edition of *Fear Factor*, I played again for the CHP families—and brought home another $10,000 for them. The other celebrities on the show—my rivals—were Stephen Baldwin, Kevin Richardson (of

the Backstreet Boys), Ali Landry (*Spy TV*), Kelly Packard
(*Baywatch*), and Alan Thicke. It was a wild ride for all of
us—so outrageous . . . so thrilling . . . so terrifying. It's the
kind of show where your heart could end up in your
throat if you're not careful.

Now, if you remember the opening moments of each
Fear Factor, there's an announcement that the stunts were
designed and supervised by professionals, and because of
their danger, they shouldn't be attempted *by anyone at any
time*. A standard disclaimer, I assume, but with at least one
of those stunts in mind, maybe I should have taken those
words to heart. I absolutely came unglued at one point—
but I'll get to that in a moment.

So many people have asked me about *Fear Factor* (and
still do!) that I'll spend a few pages telling you all about it. If
you saw the show, you may remember my opening comments, which were something like, "I don't think my fans are
going to be surprised to see me on the show, because my
character Sami Brady on *Days of Our Lives* is a villain. She
has drugged people, poisoned people, pushed people around,
and tried to choke people to death! I've done everything on
the show, so now I'm going to give it a shot in real life!"

How's that for an opening?!

Well, I'm pretty competitive. In fact, I made a comment
that the women on daytime television sometimes have a
reputation for being divas, but I was going to break that
stereotype for good and show how tough we really are!
But the other celebrities on *Fear Factor* were just as confident—or in the case of Stephen Baldwin, downright cocky
(sorry, Stephen, but it's true!). In an off-the-cuff, macho
monologue, Stephen proclaimed, "Here's the deal. I don't

even have to compete right now because I've already won!
Seriously, I might as well go take a nap, because I'm the
winner."

Stunt #1

I was absolutely determined to win the Triple Crown
on the show, and my confidence level couldn't have been
any higher when we began at the foot of a Los Angeles
skyscraper and peered up to its stratospheric, nosebleed-
level heights. Joe Rogan, the host, explained that we were
about to embark on a *Spiderman*-like stunt, climbing out
of a thirty-sixth-floor window and inching our way
around the outside of the building, tiptoeing on a narrow,
one-inch-wide window sill and using overhead handholds
along the way. We had three minutes to grab as many yel-
low flags as possible and transfer them one at a time from
the starting point to the finish line. The four contestants
who transferred the most flags in three minutes would advance to the next round. In other words, two of us would
be heading home very soon.

When it was my turn and I got up to the thirty-sixth
floor, I remember looking at the street below and thinking,
"My God, it's so far down there," but also telling myself
that I could do it. It was pretty intense. It was so challenging. The wind was blowing hard, too, which sure didn't
help. But I truly believed that I could polish this one off
with no problem. Once I was all hooked up, I stayed determined and resolute. I was completely focused on the
task at hand.

Do you remember what happened? I maneuvered on

my tiptoes during my entire time on that ledge. It was tough—real tough. After grabbing and delivering the second flag in less time than Kelly did, and giving a thumb's up to the cameraman because I knew I'd done enough to stay in the game, I suddenly lost my grip and careened into the L.A. sky. Fortunately the safety harness didn't forsake me. I dangled and bounced against the window panes on the lower floors until the crew could pull me in. It actually felt pretty cool hanging in midair, and I was so confident in the safety measures that I didn't freak when I took the plunge.

That entire experience was so amazing, so exciting, so frightening—all at the same time. I remember Kelly saying that the stunt had been so intense that her arms felt just like Jell-O. I know exactly what she meant. More than anything, my calves were killing me, as if they were on fire! Ali Landry admitted that she had said a little prayer before she stepped out onto the ledge, with the street a distant 36 floors below! But this was *Fear Factor*, and none of us expected to be able to coast through it. Kelly and Alan were eliminated and went home after that first round. When I asked Joe who in the world came up with the ideas for these insane stunts, he said, "They have a whole team of freaks!" That sums it up.

By the way, Stephen continued to talk trash throughout that first stunt, and in fact he bet all of us $100 that he would get four flags—but he didn't come close to four (he quit after only two!!). So here's my message to Stephen: "I'm still waiting for my $100, Stephen! You know where to reach me!"

Stunt #2

We moved onto the second stunt, which I'll never forget, and I do mean *never!* It still gives me the creeps just thinking about it. One by one, each of us had to lie down in a Plexiglas "coffin," which the *Fear Factor* crew had divided into three sections. From the knees down, thousands of nightcrawlers were poured onto us. Then the middle section was filled with one hundred red and white snakes. And finally (get ready for this!) our head and face were bathed in 3,000 huge Madagascar cockroaches—crawling, hissing cockroaches that were as terrifying as anything I've ever seen (or had crawling all over my face!). The game called for each of us to find and grab the white snakes swarming over our midsection, and put ten of them into a nearby bin as quickly as possible.

Well, I went first (lucky me!). Before I climbed into the box, Joe must have sensed that I was already becoming rattled, and he asked if I was OK. With my voice quivering, I said, "Of course not! You lie down in this empty thing, and then they put these f—ing bugs on your head!"

I wasn't acting. Man, I was *really* scared. Absolutely petrified.

I put on a pair of goggles, and as I stepped into the box, I was already very upset, even before the stopwatch started ticking. Stephen began singing "La Cucaracha" as all the little critters were poured on top of me (Stephen really is *crazy!*). I was wearing a pair of shorts, and I screamed and shrieked as the worms were emptied onto my legs. ("Oh, God, eeahh!") Then the snakes. Then the cockroaches. The roaches were beyond disgusting, crawling all over the place (and all over my face). I've never seen so many hyperactive bugs in my life! I was dying to get started—actually, I was just dying!—and wanted to get this miserable experience over with as quickly as possible.

"Hurry up!" I shouted. "Hurry up!"

At long last, the timer was started, and I frantically tried to find the white snakes while also slapping the crawling cockroaches away from my mouth and nose. The hissing of the roaches was so scary, and I was starting to lose it. Shouting. Shaking. Panicking. I was a real mess. With those cockroaches all over me, I had definitely met my personal "fear factor."

Finally, I got ten snakes off my midsection and into the bin. My time: 1:54.

At that moment, however, I really didn't care what my time was. I just wanted to escape from that "coffin." *Really* quickly. I began screaming for help in getting me out of the box, but I had to wait until all the snakes and other creatures were removed. So there I was for a few more seconds, with only the cockroaches to keep me company! I began pleading, "Get me out of here! Get me out! NOW!" My shouts were ear-splitting.

Ali Landry was holding my hand and telling me, "Just breathe!" Joe was trying to calm me down, too, saying "Nothing bad is happening to you. It just feels gross. You're fine!"

"Please hurry!" I shouted. "I'm about to seriously FREAK OUT!! Get me out of here!!"

My motor was really racing. Finally, all the snakes were removed and I flew out of the coffin; I could have made the Olympic high jumping team with that leap. I mean, I was so close to totally flipping out. Once I was on solid ground, I hopped in the air a few times, trying to slap any remaining creatures off of me.

That was so petrifying. It took me a few minutes to regain even a bit of composure. I mean it, I was coming out of my skin.

Ali Landry held my hand, and said, "I've never seen anybody freak out like that in my life!" Trying to catch my breath, I remained pretty flustered and shaken for a while, and mumbled, "Those cockroaches are the most disgusting thing I have ever felt crawling all over my face. Oh, my God! . . . You think you have an idea of how creepy it's going to be—it's maybe 150 times worse!"

Joe seemed stunned by my reaction. "This is the most freaked out I've ever seen anyone on the show." Maybe he was right.

Frankly, I could barely watch the others going through the same stunt. I began to get anxious all over again just seeing the crew pour the bugs and the snakes on Ali. She admitted later that she was afraid of snakes, and she ended up with a scratch on her nose from the cockroaches. But through it all, she stayed pretty calm. Tears came to my eyes while I watched her grab the snakes, one by one, and toss them into the bin. I backed into a corner, crossed my arms over my chest, and tried to keep it together. I admit it, I was bonkers by that point.

Unfortunately for me, all of the other players got their ten snakes into the bin faster than I did. Stephen's time was something like one minute flat! I was crushed by finishing last. I just figured that I had done my best but would be on my way home—and after that experience, I thought maybe it was time!

But then Joe made me an offer. "Ali, since we're playing

for charity, if you eat one of these roaches, you can go into the finals." He also promised me that if I ate a roach, he would, too!

Oh, no. Was he kidding? On the one hand, I was excited by the chance to move onto the next round. But I could still hear the roaches hissing. And I started to freak out all over again. I told Joe, "Dude"—(I say "dude" a lot; I'm a Valley girl!)—"Dude, I can't believe you offered me this!"

As I collected my thoughts, I made him a counteroffer. I proposed eating a worm instead of a cockroach. (I have my dad to thank for my negotiating skills!) Joe and I finally settled on me eating three worms—and Joe still eating the cockroach.

"I can't believe I'm doing this," I said. "This is so wrong!" I remember wondering if eating the worms would be bad for my health. I also didn't want to throw up on national television!

The others were egging me on ("This is for your charity, Ali"). So I bounced the worms from one hand to the other for a few moments, then covered my nose and popped the worms in, one by one. Yes, three very wiggly worms. Three very slimy worms.

This is the question I always get—"What did the worms taste like?" Oh, God, they were disgusting! I chewed them as quickly as possible, feeling their nasty, sour juice squirting into my mouth (sorry if that was a little graphic, but it's true!!). I leaped into the air with disgust. I coughed. I gagged. I desperately wanted to put this horrible experience behind me.

Finally, it was done. But it took me a while to recover from that one. A long while. I don't know what I would have done if Joe hadn't agreed to the "three-worm deal" instead of the cockroach. Meanwhile, as he had promised, Joe did eat one of the cockroaches, with each noisy crunch echoing off the walls. He looked like he might lose his lunch, but he got through it. I'm not sure I would have!

Meanwhile, Stephen Baldwin saw me go through all of this, and was stunned by what he had witnessed. Later, here's what he said, word for word:

> *"This show is totally insane! Alison Sweeney is whacked! Sweeney's the one I'm worried about now. If you can freak like that, come back and eat three worms, anything's possible! That was one of the sexiest things I saw in my life!"*

I guess that was a compliment. With Stephen, you never know.

By the way, after the cameras were turned off, I chucked up whatever was in my stomach, including the worms. I didn't want to have nightmares, wondering what was crawling through my stomach that night!

Stunt #3

By comparison, the third and final stunt was a breeze. We had to enter a steel cage, which was then padlocked and lowered into a large tank of cold water. Our challenge: Grab a ring of keys, find the right key to unlock the cage, throw open the door and swim to the surface and to a nearby buoy. Stephen went first, and he was pretty awesome. He completed the stunt in an incredible twenty-four seconds. He was moving so fast and so frantically that he cracked his head on the cage and was bleeding from the forehead when he came to the surface of the water. But twenty-four seconds—that would be tough to beat. Yet I still felt confident.

Kevin Richardson fumbled and groped with the keys and lost his chance of winning (his time: forty-three seconds). Ali Landry was next, and seemed to panic once she was underwater and the keys didn't work right away. After a few moments, she jettisoned herself through the cage's emergency exit and was disqualified (while the safety divers came to her rescue).

Then it was my turn. I stepped into the cage, gave the thumbs up, and was lowered into the tank I began working quickly. After just a few seconds, I had opened the lock. With still a little time to spare, I swam furiously to the surface, but made a fatal error: I hadn't thought about where the buoy was when I came out of the cage. I burst through the surface of the water, but had no idea which way to swim. After a few more precious seconds passed, I finally splashed my way to the buoy. My time: twenty-nine seconds—five more seconds than Stephen. He won $50,000 for his charity; I won $10,000 for mine.

After all was said and done, Stephen was still shaking his head. Going into the last stunt, he remained steadfast that I was the only one he was worried about. "If you can bug out, recover, come back, eat three worms, that's hardcore! Alison, I think you're terrific. I think you're a rock-solid righteous chick!" Then he added, "Win or lose, this kid is what it's all about!"

That was nice of Stephen to say. But, Stephen, you still owe me $100, buddy!!

Looking back, I'm so proud of getting through all three

stunts (especially the second one!). I can't say I loved *every* minute of it (think worms and cockroaches!). But I'd do it again if they asked me to! My time spent bonding with the cockroaches was later repeated on *Fear Factor*'s "Best Of" show, featured as one of the program's most outrageous moments! The executive producer of *Fear Factor*, Matt Kunitz, put it this way: "Alison Sweeney is one of my all-time favorite *Fear Factor* contestants. Even though she was horrified and gave us one of our most outrageous 'fear' moments, she finished the stunt and proved that fear was not a factor for her!"

Chapter 17

Show business is in my blood. I'm sure you've figured that out by now. Even though I've been an actress almost all of my life, I hope that in terms of the length of my career, I'm barely out of the starting blocks, and that this is only the beginning.

Since I've been on *Days of Our Lives*, I've received more awards than I ever could have imagined. As I write these words, I've won the *Soap Opera Digest* Award four times, as well as the Breakout Performer of the Year Award from *Soap Opera Weekly*, and the Best Bad Girl Award from *Inside Soap* (the Australian magazine). My head is still spinning from the twenty-ninth Annual Daytime Emmy Awards in 2002, where the fans themselves voted me an Emmy as America's Favorite Villain. (For all of you who cast your votes for me on the Internet, I'm still saying "thank you"!)

Those awards sure mean a lot to me—just being nomi-nated is such an honor—but with my schedule and the de-

(JPI Studios, Inc.)

With the cast of *Days* at the TV Guide Awards

mands on my time often so unpredictable, I've sometimes
made those awards programs a little more tense and exciting than they need to be. I'll never forget my first *Soap
Opera Digest* Awards show, where my older brother Sten
was my date. We were running so late (my fault, not his!),
and when we finally arrived, the ushers rushed us in, right
at the moment my award was announced! I had barely sat
down when my name was called as the winner, and I had
to get right back up and accept my award. I was a little out
of breath and a bit frazzled when I reached the stage, but
fortunately my acceptance speech was coherent and resembled the English language for the most part, and I somehow remembered to thank everyone who I wanted to
thank. Everything worked out, but what a close call! By
the way, I'd like to be able to tell you that I learned my lesson that year, and that ever since I've been punctual for the

annual show—but that would be a lie! I've been late to every *Soap Opera Digest* Award show when I've been a nominee—yes, every one of them—and I'm sure I've raised the blood pressure of the show's producers as the clock ticked and they wondered where in the heck Alison Sweeney was—again! When I've been only a presenter on the show, the pressure's been off, and I've always breezed in with time to spare, ready to hit my mark. But as a nominee, the award show "curse" seems to take me over, and being a late arrival has become something of a way of life. Go figure . . .

Fortunately, critics don't write reviews about showing up late to awards shows, and in fact, I've been lucky to have gotten some fabulous reviews over the years for my acting, although I'm the first to give much of the credit to my talented fellow actors on *Days*. I remember when I read a critique in *Soap Opera Digest* that said, "Sweeney holds her own with the best of them on *Days of Our Lives*, including powerhouse Deidre Hall." Of course, I'm enormously flattered by comments like that. But I know that so much of the praise should go to Deidre and the rest of the cast of *Days*, who have supported me and helped me develop as an actress for more than a decade.

Even more important than the critics, however, are the fans. They're the ones who keep me inspired, who show up at events at NBC or at shopping malls and ask for autographs or for a few moments just to say hello. In June 2003, I took part in a wild and long weekend in Nashville where fourteen of us from *Days of Our Lives* and *Passions* attended the County Music Association Fan Fair, where we mingled with fans for the weekend, attended parties (including a crazy one at the Wild Horse), and signed autographs until well past the time when writers' cramp set in. I must have had way too much fun, because after I got back to Los Angeles I couldn't talk for *four days*! Coincidentally, Sami had a throat injury at the same time on the show, too, so the fans never heard my raw vocal cords.

Sami is so much fun for me to play. In some ways, she's a young woman who never really grew up fully. From the first day I began playing her, one of her driving motivations has been to have her parents (Roman and Marlena) be together again. She has always wanted—and always lacked—the love and security of a family unit. She has seen the woman she has become, and blames the shortcomings she sees in herself on the absence of a happy, healthy home life. She is a very complex and always a very interesting character to play.

With each passing year, I've become more comfortable playing Sami, and I've brought more of myself into my character. Subtleties in my own personality and characteristics get incorporated into Sami. I often interject my sense of humor and facial expressions into Sami when it's appropriate. I've always been an animated talker, but when I play Sami, I sometimes go over the top with the way that Sami reacts to the world around her (after all, she is an over-the-top character, isn't she?). And by the way, there's much less Sami in Ali than the other way around (thank goodness!). She's a character who laughs and cries, who loves and hates to the extreme, which is what makes her so interesting.

As for the fans, they continue to feel empathy for Sami one moment, and despise her the next. And it's totally understandable, based on her behavior. She often does the right thing, and she certainly cares about her son. She's also very insecure, and a lot of people can relate to that. Viewers sometimes tell me that they see something of themselves in her. But Sami is also so spiteful and malicious at times that you can't help but hate the hell-raising side of her. When her evil nature surfaces, I know she drives fans absolutely mad! But even after she's been embarrassed and humiliated—and sometimes it gets *really* bad—Sami always picks herself up, dusts herself off, and gets on with life. And that's pretty admirable.

Here's one letter I received not long ago:

> *I love to act, and I would love to get a spot on a soap opera. And who knows, maybe I could end up playing the bitch! I can't wait to see the next show and see what scheme Sami is cooking up next! I love you as an actress; you add that extra special spice to the show. Keep doing what you're doing because you're awesome at it!*
>
> *Your loyal fan,*
> *Heather*

An Unexpected Visitor

As I mentioned earlier, I can get a little star-struck, too. But probably nothing compared to a very memorable recent moment on the *Days* set, when I had a completely unexpected "celebrity sighting." It occurred one afternoon just before Thanksgiving in 2003. We were dry blocking, and Steve Wyman (our co-executive producer) was directing the show that day. I was off-stage at that moment, waiting to make my entrance, when I glanced to my right—and couldn't believe my eyes. Shaquille O'Neal was stepping out of the shadows, and walking in my general direction.

Well, I'm a huge basketball fan—and as it turned out, Shaq is a big *Days* fan. He was on the NBC lot to appear on the *Tonight Show*, and while waiting for his taping to

(Author's personal collection)

start, he wandered over to the *Days* set. When I caught sight of him, I was absolutely astounded. It's not every day you bump into a 7-foot-1, 340-pound basketball superstar! I rushed over to him and introduced myself while desperately trying to keep my cool. He was so friendly, and as we found out, his wife watches *Days* all the time, and that's how Shaq got introduced to the show.

I wanted to stay and talk with Shaq, but I had to get back to work, darn it. But let me tell you, I was so overwhelmed for a few moments. Other *Days* cast members told me that I was blushing, and I began fanning myself with my script to try to regain my composure.

During the dry blocking, I kept glancing over as Shaq was being given a mini-tour of the set. I tried to pay attention to my work but it was hard. Then I saw that other cast members were getting their photo taken with him, and—well, this was an opportunity I couldn't pass up. I finally said to Steve, "Can I *please* go take a picture with Shaq?"

Steve must have thought I was crazy, but he said, "Sure, go ahead."

That photo with Shaq is one of my all-time favorites. He had his arm around my shoulder, and it just about enveloped my entire upper body. He is so huge!!

The Road to the Future

As I look ahead, I have all kinds of goals for myself. Playing Sami for so many years has been unbelievable. Even though I've been portraying the same character for so long, Sami has changed and grown in a million different ways—and yet she's still the same person at heart (and sometimes that heart is pretty sinister!). But as Sami has evolved, it has given me a chance to develop as an actress as well.

Of course, playing Sami is *never* boring, thanks to escapades like kidnappings, tampering with paternity tests, drugging her older sister's fiancé, trying to sell her baby sister on the black market, and facing her own execution on Death Row. It certainly doesn't remind you of the Waltons, does it?

I'm used to the pace of performing in a one-hour soap every day, but it can still be a challenge. There are thirty pages of dialogue to read and learn each day (I still occasionally have nightmares about forgetting all my lines!). There are early calls that leave no room for sleeping in or idling away the morning hours (6:45 A.M. tomorrow morning as I write this!), and there's certainly no time or tolerance for feeling full of yourself, self-centered, or bigheaded. Fortunately, I've always had a strong work ethic, and that keeps me focused on what needs to be done, day after day, one show after another.

Because *Days* continues to keep me so busy, it's hard for me to find much time for other acting jobs, like guest-starring roles on situation comedies or TV movies of the week. When I was a kid, I went to a lot of auditions and I just loved it (in prekindergarten I jabbered so much—telling random stories whenever I spoke in class—that my teacher finally told my mom, "You know, your daughter talks so much; why don't you take her on auditions and let her make some money from all that chatter?!").

Today, I try to make auditions from time to time, but I work so much on *Days*, I often don't feel it's the best use of my down time to spend three hours at an audition, particularly the so-called "cattle calls" where a hundred actresses may be chasing the same role.

Yes, I do have breaks in the *Days* taping schedule now and then, but they don't occur with the kind of regularity that makes it possible to do much advance planning. It's hard enough to arrange a doctor's appointment, much less prepare for an audition! I've come to terms with the fact that if I'm not going to get to most auditions, that's okay. I'm not going to let myself stress out over it because scheduling conflicts make it impossible for me to be there, or because I've gotten stuck in an L.A. traffic jam that means I'll never make it on time. If it's something beyond my control, it's not worth freaking out over it.

As you can see, I'm working on keeping my life and my psyche in balance. Yes, I still have many, many days when I'm extremely busy at NBC. But I'm also doing better at becoming grounded, and finding time not only for work but also for family and friends. I've found that when I put too much emphasis on one part of my life—or when I exaggerate the importance of one event over another—it does nothing for my well-being, either physically or emotionally.

As I've told you throughout this book, very early in life I was unusually lucky to discover the career I wanted to pursue. I dreamed of being an actress from the age of four, and I always believed that I would succeed. But while I seemed to have my act together in front of the camera, I was brimming with insecurities inside. I've had to find out who I am and what makes me happy. My life experiences have provided me with insights and the confidence to strive even harder toward my goals.

Not long ago, I showed up for an audition. I read my lines and thought I did pretty well. But apparently the director didn't agree. Another actress got the part—and what did I get from the director? Nothing but a nasty comment or two. Yes, I was bummed out on the drive home. But then I made a conscious decision not to dwell on it and let it ruin my evening. I shook it off and went out to a movie with Dave. I refused to let one person's negative opinion undermine my usually positive frame of mind. It's not worth it, whether it lasts an hour, a day, or much longer. I'm not going to give it more importance than it deserves—not when I have much more significant people and things to take care of in my life, whether it's having a quiet dinner with my husband, or simply enjoying happiness wherever it appears.

For the long term, I'd not only like to build upon my skills as an actress, but (as I mentioned earlier) I also hope to direct someday. Yes, I know what you're thinking: Doesn't *every* actor in Hollywood want to direct? But this is a path that I'm determined to pursue in the future. There have been times when I've felt that there must be some dark comedies out there waiting for me to direct (that's where my own sense of humor lies!).

I've actually been traveling along the learning curve toward becoming a director for years now. On the set of *Days*, I'm constantly watching our own directors at work and I've taken volumes of mental notes. When opportunities present themselves, I've asked our directors one question after another, and I've learned so much about the creative process from them. They have such enormous talent and so much responsibility, and I've taken every chance to learn from them. And they've been so generous with their time and their expertise.

Fan Feedback

If you haven't already done so, I hope you'll begin spending time on my website: *www.alisonsweeney.com* (at last count, there are about 26,000 unique new visitors to my website each week, and I hope you'll join them). It's a great way to stay in touch and keep up to date on recent happenings in my life and my upcoming personal appearances. One of my favorite parts of being an actress on an afternoon TV show is hearing from and communicating with fans who always seem to have an opinion about what Sami's been up to. I hope you'll drop me a letter or an e-mail from time to time and let me know your ideas about some of the issues I've discussed in this book, as well as what you think about Sami's latest escapades. I read every letter and answer as many of them as possible.

I'd also like to hear about your own life, your own goals, and how you're working to turn them into reality. I hope this book has inspired you to follow your desires and your heart, and to make the most of the years ahead. I certainly don't claim to be an authority or to have the answer for every question. But as I've spoken to and received letters from so many fans, I realize that there are a thousand ways to make the journey and pursue your dreams, whether your goals are to have a fantastic career, build meaningful relationships, manage your weight, improve your fitness, or simply to find happiness in the world.

Over time, I'm achieving more happiness and more peace of mind. No, I don't have a perfect life. But I've discovered a way of living that works for me. I've come to accept and love myself, no matter what the achievements and setbacks in my career may be . . . no matter how many friends I have . . . no matter what problems I may be facing . . . no matter how much I weigh. The number on the scale, for example, certainly doesn't change who I am; I don't take it personally anymore.

I encourage you to find your own path to happiness and fulfillment. As much as possible, live more in rhythm with the person who you really are and want to become. Listen to your heart and your inner voice, and strive for a life that you find rewarding and meaningful.

In the role of Sami Brady, I did break the mold and the stereotype of what a daytime TV character should be like. I didn't necessarily have to be the nicest, the thinnest, the most secure, or the most popular person in the world for fans to like me.

If it suits you, I'd like to see you break the mold, too. Remember, you can be happy and healthy, even if you don't fit the stereotype of perfection (which *none* of us really does). You don't need to be perfect to have a successful life. You just need to be yourself.

Thank you again to my many fans who have supported me through my life.

Stick around—the plan is for it to keep getting better.

Afterword

Soap 101

There are tons of rumors about *Days of Our Lives* on the Internet and just about everywhere else. For instance, I always find it so entertaining when fans come up with crazy theories and assumptions each time actors leave the show. Were they fired? Or did they leave by choice? Did they have major disagreements with the producers? Did the writers find them difficult to work with? Was money an issue?

There is a lot of fan curiosity about every aspect of the show. In this Afterword, let me address some of the issues that fans most often ask about. Throughout this book, I've already described much of what goes on behind the scenes and on the set. But let me spend a few more pages describing the exciting life and hectic pace of being an actor on *Days*.

When an actor joins a soap, the standard contract is for

three years, and the first contract is broken into thirteen-week cycles. This means that while the actor commits to the producer for three years, the producer reserves the right to fire the actor every thirteen weeks (in subsequent contracts, the 13-week cycles may be replaced by twenty-six-week periods). In the contract, the actor is also guaranteed a minimum number of episodes that he'll appear in during every 13-week cycle, and the actor gets paid in full, even for episodes that were promised but never materialized. If the producer decides to terminate the actor's contract at the end of a thirteen-week cycle, the actor has to be notified six weeks before his or her tenure on the show ends.

I've been fortunate to be on *Days* since I was sixteen years old—more than a decade now. And as I've mentioned earlier in the book, we have a very cohesive, tightly knit cast, with none of the cutthroat atmosphere you hear about on other shows. There's no competition for so-called "front-burner" vs. "back-burner" story lines because the writers constantly cycle all the characters so each of us has our moments to be front and center with one story line or another. You have to be patient, but everyone's opportunity comes up with regularity.

The *Days* actors aren't on the set everyday—only on those days where our characters are in the episode being taped. So we sometimes find ourselves with two to three days off a week, but with little advance notice. We may get our schedules two weeks (or sometimes less) ahead of time, so trying to schedule a dentist's appointment or a long weekend getaway is often a fly-by-the-seat-of-our-pants experience.

The producers are contractually obligated to give each

actor two weeks of vacation a year, but they're not necessarily the two weeks you want, and most certainly not two weeks in a row. You better ask way in advance if there's a particular week you want to travel to a family reunion or wedding, for example. With advance notice, the scripts can be shaped to work around your absence. Or the producers may pre-tape your scenes so your character never misses an episode and the audience never knows you're gone.

The show goes on hiatus two weeks a year at Christmas. Everyone gets those two weeks off. To make that possible, we tape ten extra episodes a year—usually six episodes in a five-day period, or sometimes we work Saturdays to create a backlog of extra shows so we can spend the two weeks at Christmas with our families.

Before the actors see the scripts, of course, the writers have spent a lot of time creating and fine-tuning every word. Our head writer—Jim Reilly—as well as the outline writers and the dialogue writers all take their turns sharpening each script before it ends up in the actors' laps.

At *Days*, our writers are very receptive to input from the actors, and not just when we feel that our character would say a particular line a little differently. At times, the dialogue writer may not have a comprehensive picture of our character's history or a total recall of what may have happened to our character on an episode he or she didn't work on.

I remember one episode revolving around one of Sami's "non-weddings" to Austin, and I had a huge two-page monologue to memorize, where Sami pleads with Austin not to tell her family about the terrible things she had done that made Austin want to break up with her before reaching the altar. In the script, Sami recaps the difficult life she has led in a plea for sympathy from Austin, and in hopes that he and her family would not judge her too harshly.

I memorized this entire two-page monologue (not to mention the rest of the episode, which had plenty of Sami dialogue), and when I arrived on the set on Monday to shoot the scene, Drake Hogestyn told me, "I'm sorry, Ali, this script is all wrong—you can't say some of these lines because that's not what happened. This isn't what took place in Sami's childhood on the show."

Well, I wasn't on *Days* when my character was a little kid, and there had been some very complicated story lines that were there before my time. Drake was around for those early episodes, and so he made a lot of suggestions for revisions.

We were so grateful that Drake had caught these errors. But after spending the entire weekend memorizing my monologue, I had about ten minutes to change gears and memorize the hurriedly revised script! To make my task even more difficult, I was just memorizing words, and had no visual context to put them in. In general, to help me learn my lines, I can usually call on *Days* scenes that I remember from the past, and I can use them to assist me in committing the new lines to memory. But this new task was a real challenge. Eventually, it was mission accomplished, but it wasn't easy!

At times, mistakes do slip by everyone—except the fans, that is. One year at Christmas, Sami had a line where she said, "I hate egg nog!" Well, in a scene the following year, I carried some egg nog and poured it into a glass in the background of a scene. And leave it to our fans! I got a letter from a viewer who remembered that Sami hated egg nog! I guess our fans are our ultimate fact-checkers.

I know that I'll never lose sight of the fans and how important they are to the success of the show. Yes, we often work very hard and very long hours. But none of us has anything to complain about. It's a great job, and it's so wonderful being part of the lives of our millions of viewers five days a week. I'm a very lucky person—and I know it.